NATIONAL INTEREST AND NATIONAL SECURITY

POLICY-MAKING PRISM FOR INDIA

NATIONAL INTEREST AND NATIONAL SECURITY POLICY-MAKING PRISM FOR INDIA

GAUTAM SEN

KW
KNOWLEDGE WORLD

KW Publishers Pvt Ltd
New Delhi

Centre for Land Warfare Studies
Delhi Cantt
New Delhi

The Centre for Land Warfare Studies (CLAWS), New Delhi, is an autonomous think tank dealing with contemporary issues of national security and conceptual aspects of land warfare, including conventional and sub-conventional conflicts and terrorism. CLAWS conducts research that is futuristic in outlook and policy-oriented in approach.

Centre for Land Warfare Studies
RPSO Complex, Parade Road, Delhi Cantt, New Delhi 110010
Tel: +91.11.25691308 **Fax:** +91.11.25692347
Email: landwarfare@gmail.com **Website:** www.claws.in
CLAWS Army No. 33098

ISBN   978-93-86288-51-6   Paperback
ISBN   978-93-86288-52-3   ebook

Published in India by
Kalpana Shukla
KW Publishers Pvt Ltd
4676/21, First Floor, Ansari Road, Daryaganj, New Delhi 110002
Tel: +91.11.23263498 / 43528107 **Email:** knowledgeworld@kwpub.com
Website: www.kwpub.com

2011 BEST PUBLISHERS AWARD (ENGLISH)

Printed and bound in India

CONTENTS

NATIONAL INTEREST AND NATIONAL SECURITY POLICY-MAKING PRISM FOR INDIA

Preamble

The national security strategy is an integral part of a nation-state's quest to safeguard its national interest. Today, nation-states comprise the unit of analysis of international relations amongst them, bilaterally and multilaterally, at regional and global levels. National interest involves the securitisation of a nation from external and internal threats by synergising with foreign policy-making to ensure that diplomacy plays a complementary as well as supporting role to meet the goals and objectives of national interest. This synergisation leads to the evolution of a structured architecture of the national security policy-making prism which is institutionalised in such a way as to incorporate the ideas and roles of all the stakeholders in a democratic form of governance.

India, as the largest democracy in the world, has proved the structural, intellectual, moral and social efficacy of a functional democratic system over the past 70 years. Though its national security policy-making has been disjointed,[1] it has remained functional in times of crisis. Therefore, the problems related to India's national security policy-making require an in-depth study of the problems of the cultural and civilisational preconditions in a multi-dimensional perspective in which the various components of social science disciplines must come together for the formulation of a unified theoretical orientation.

The problems of national security for a country like India, which has experienced a series of catastrophes from within and a continuing threat from without, has to be formulated in terms of the larger goals and aspirations to which this civilisational community has committed itself. In essence, India can think of three main objectives. First, national stability and integrity; second, social political and economic progress; and third, peace and stability in terms of its relationships with other states, regionally and globally.

Therefore, India's national security as an essential component to securitise its national interest must be seen in terms of these larger goals. If this may be called the cultural dimension of the problems of national security, then one has to look at the political perspectives as well. Here we have to consider a complex interaction between our perceptions of our neighbours beyond the borders as well as the larger major powers, and their perceptions and assessments of our situation and our objectives.

It is within this matrix of relationships that the specific goals of India's defence policy will get structured. The cultural and political aspects of the problems create a texture of tasks and priorities of decision-making and possible options for actions. The actualisation of objectives as modulated and structured requires an adequate process of institutionalisation, ranging from the economic to the administrative and legal preconditions. This institutionalisation[2] of national security efforts itself creates further problems and difficulties. Hence, all three dimensions viz. the cultural, socio-political and institutional are involved in a complex interaction calling for skills and patterns of leadership at all levels of the problems. Therefore, we have a final dimension of how various forms of leadership may be required to respond creatively to the complexities of the problem. In this whole endeavour, the role of all the stakeholders as given in the schematic diagram of the national security policy-making prism becomes normatively essential. Hence, a clear articulation of the various facets of the situation, their complex relationships and also a sharp awareness of the possible contributions, tensions and pressures that must be overcome, as well as the contributions of scholars in the cultural and philosophical disciplines will be needed to examine the normative aspects of the problems of security in the light of ideals to which India is committed e.g. the neo-liberal dimensions of non-alignment, national security, social justice and global peace.

The framework of the analysis is in three parts:

Part I: **Contextualising National Interest for National Security Strategy**

Part II: **The Theoretical Moorings of India's Foreign Policy-Making**

Part III: **The National Security Policy-Making Prism: The Indian Context**

PART 1

CONTEXTUALISING NATIONAL INTEREST FOR NATIONAL SECURITY STRATEGY

Introduction

The national security strategy is an integral part of a nation-state's quest to safeguard its national interest. Today, nation-states comprise the unit of analysis of international relations amongst them, bilaterally and multilaterally, at regional and global levels.

International affairs and international relations today have tabulated 67 theories[3] to answer the questions related to security, national security and human rights which are still in a stage of transformation, transition and, many times, without any answers. The study of International Relations (IR) in the past and even in the 21st century remains embedded in studying the behaviour of states and the ever-expanding issues on security and human rights. The debate remained unfinished all through the period of the Cold War. Kolodziej, in his critique of Stephen Waltz's survey of security studies, identified serious flaws in the understanding of security studies, viewed from the analytic, normative and methodological perspectives. Kolodziej emphasised on a more enriched conceptual and larger interdisciplinary, theoretically more inclusive and more policy-oriented understanding of security studies[4] rather than pursuing a policy relevant approach, as suggested by Waltz's survey in 1991.[5]

Here it is necessary to address two issues interrelated to each other: national security strategy and national interest. However, if one looks at the issues normatively, they do not exist in compartments but are interrelated as well as interdependent. Therefore, it will be correct to touch upon the broad contours of each of the two issues. Identifying the challenges of the 21st century globally brings forth the issues of comprehensive security, within which the issue of the national security of individual nation-states is ensconced. As a student of strategy, one is naturally overtaken every time by looking through the conceptual lenses of conflict, peace and conflict resolution.

IR Challenges and National Security Strategy

The Theoretical Construct
Conceptually, one can identify two main theories, which explain the post Cold War world liberalism and realism. Liberalism and proponents of liberal persuasion like Francis Fukuyama, a former US State Department official, an expert

on Third World politics, shot into prominence by writing one of the most effective articles entitled "End of History"[6] in 1989. His thesis consisted of a set of assertions. These assertions were, first, that history, since the end of the French Revolution has been driven by the core dynamic conflict between the forces supporting collectivism and those endorsing 'bourgeois' individualism; second, with the Russian revolution in 1917, the balance began to tilt toward 'collectivism'; and, third, by the late 1970s, the tilt began to go towards 'individualism' as the various efforts at economic planning in the Third World started to 'show signs of fatigue'. This was seen more prominently in the Soviet Union after Gorbachev assumed office in 1985, and began to challenge the former Soviet assumptions. Gorbachev finally abandoned Eastern Europe, and the people of those states opted for 'bourgeois' democracy and market economics Thus, the Cold War ended on terms favourable to the West. This, according to Fukuyama, was a victory for the forces of individualism, and he termed this point of time as the 'end' of one phase of history and the beginning of another wherein liberal economic values would prevail globally. Hence, there was no alternative to 'bourgeois democracy' taking over globally. This view was supported by three key liberal arguments. The first was to do with democracy in the Kantian sense, which, in essence, stated that while authoritarianism bred war, democracies ushered in peace. Hence, the greater the number of democracies, the more were the chances of a peaceful world. This assertion was linked with another hypothesis concerning the role of institutions. This notion asserted that this also helped to organise the world in a more efficient way by mediating in conflicts between states. This, in turn, supported the third hypothesis that by overcoming the logic of anarchy, the cause of peace rested on the existence of capitalism. While the liberals did not underestimate the dark side of capitalism, they argued that as world trade grew, financial interdependence between different geographical areas and countries would result in greater investment in each other's economies. This would create a strong incentive for states to get on with each other. While the possibility of conflict remained in an integrated economic system, the likelihood of conflict would naturally diminish dramatically.

While the liberals painted a peaceful world, the realists painted a bleaker picture. They saw much more of chaos and conflict occurring because the international system continues to remain competitive and anarchic, and past history showed the failures of building new world orders (like after the end of World War I) or the assessment of the world as it became after 1989, with all the barbaric wars, failed states and collapsing regions. Hence, the inference was that there was nothing to be too optimistic about. The three main political thinkers of the realist school to challenge the liberals were John Mearsheimer, Professor of political science in the University of Chicago, Robert D Kaplan, and Samuel Huntington of Harvard University. Mearsheimer concentrated on the analysis of the structure of the international system during the Cold War in line with Kenneth Waltz's thesis on bipolarity which produced stability in the post World War II and, therefore, its collapse could generate new problems, especially it could further nuclear proliferation as the most dangerous one. Mearsheimer also postulated that the division of Europe and Germany after 1946, had created a new continental order and, hence, the unification of both would usher in uncertainty. He argued that with the collapse of Communism in the East, old ethnic hatreds would resurface to thrust the continent back into chaos and bloodshed.

Kaplan, in his study of the Cold War, worked on the assumption that economics and human collapse in parts of Africa were relevant to our understanding of the future character of world politics. Kaplan felt that in this real world, old structures and traditional certainties were fast disappearing, producing chaos and misery. Samuel Huntington, the third scholar from Harvard, placed realism in the forefront of the post Cold War debate. He warned about the world after 1989. He refuted the liberal argument by stating that the world now faced the Cold War clash of secular economic ideologies, which meant no end to conflict as such. He postulated that conflict would assume a new form defined as a 'clash of civilisations'— the evolution of conflict in the modern world. He argued that this conflict would be between the West and those other countries and regions of the world that did not adhere to values such as respect for the individual, human rights, democracy and secularism. Identity and culture were, thus, the core issues to create antagonism and they would form the new faultline in the post-Cold War world, pitting nations in Western Europe and the USA which embodied one form of 'civilisation' against those in the Middle East, China and Asia, post-Communist Russia, where the value system was profoundly different. He even warned the West that unless the West recognised this reality, it would be unable to deal with it wisely.

Global Trends
It is interesting to note that since the beginning of the 21st century, a series of reports on the global trends have been published. They are comprehensive and elaborate in nature. Global Trends 2010 was released in 1997 and the latest Global Strategic Trends 2040, is a comprehensive view of the future produced by a research team at the Development, Concepts

and Doctrine Centre (DCDC). This edition of Global Strategic Trends is benchmarked at January 12, 2010. A PPT related to Global Trends 2025 is attached in the end notes.[7] The report indicates both the strategic and non-strategic dimensions of human security in a multi-dimensional format. These trend reports are windows to the challenges that international relations will face in the 21st century. The key trends in the post Cold War era are:

- Globalisation of capitalism.
- The US – from decline to hegemony.
- Russia –reform or decline.
- China – a regional threat.
- European integration, expansion and paralysis.
- 9/11 and after.
- Migration.

Challenges in the 21st Century

The major challenges that international relations face in the 21st century are:

- Emerging new global order.
- Terrorism.
- Nuclear proliferation.
- Post-Cold War humanitarian intervention.

Emerging New Global Order?

There are two questions that need to be addressed. The first is: has there emerged a specific pattern of global order in the post-Cold War period and, if so, what are the principle constituents? The second is whether this order is to be defined in terms of globalisation?

There is obviously a pattern in the new international politics in the post-Cold War stage as compared to the one that existed prior to the end of the Cold War. The second question leads us to understand whether this contemporary order can be ensconced within globalisation. There is a major debate raging on this to understand its exact meaning, and on the process of globalisation. However, what is beyond doubt is that some kind of transformation is already under way. It is, hence, to be fathomed as to how it is to be discerned and what this will mean in practice.

Serious study to determine the overall character of the post-Cold War order is still in its infancy. We do not know how it will culminate. It is still not an 'enclosed' period with a determinate ending like in the case of the period between the two World Wars. This makes it difficult to assign particular characteristics. While there have been individual aspects of the present order (ethnicity, identity, peacekeeping, humanitarian intervention, globalisation, integration, financial instability, terrorism and the war against it, weapons of mass destruction, regime change, etc.), there is still lack of any general evaluation of its essential nature. In the earlier period, the interest in the international order was largely 'negative' and lay in ensuring that no threats emerged from it. Today, there is a high level of integration and interdependence and, hence, the interest is 'positive' which makes the international order act as a great provider of a large number of social goods. The international order today can deliver information, access to global social movements, economic resources, human rights, interventions, action through non-governmental organisations, at national and international levels, and sharing of cultural artifacts.

It will be important to state that the new order which is unfolding is being pulled in a number of different directions. At one end of the spectrum, it continues to be largely state-centric, concerned with the structure of the balance of power, the polarity of the international system and the current form of collective security. At the other end is a widening agenda of order, which encompasses the relationship between the economic and political dimensions, new thinking about human security, examining the consequences of globalisation, human rights, and environmental security. In an address to Congress on September 11, 1990, President George Bush spoke about his vision of the New World Order as follows:

> A new era, freer from the threat of terror, stronger in pursuit of justice and more secure in quest for peace, an era in which the nations of the world.... can prosper – a world where the rule of the law supplants the rule of the jungle, a world in which nations recognize the shared responsibilities for freedom and justice, a world where the strong respect the rights of the weak.

Hence, it is difficult as yet to make out the characteristics of the contemporary world order because we live in the midst of it, thus, making it hard to get a historical perspective.

Terrorism

Terrorism has emerged as a major challenge to the emerging new world order.[8] Terrorism is characterised first and foremost by the use of violence. Such violence occurs in the form of hostage taking, bombing and hijacking and other indiscriminate attacks on civilian targets. One can observe four different types of terrorist organisations: left wing terrorists, right wing terrorists, ethno-nationalist/separatist terrorists and religious terrorists. During the era of transnational terrorism, the technologies associated with globalisation by the use of communication technologies, capabilities to use physical technologies to move to great distances, communicate with and coordinate, individual or multiple attacks in different countries simultaneously, ability to retain coordination in the face of tactical setbacks, and capacity to obtain advanced weapons to conduct attacks have given a lethal capability to terrorists across regions and theatres of operation. However, it is not clear as yet as to why terrorists have not acquired and used radiological, biological or chemical weapons so far. Experts believe that terrorists understand that the more lethal their attacks are, the greater is the likelihood that a state or international community will focus all efforts on hunting them down, and eradicate them. Terrorism, however, seen as the darker side of globalisation, will continue to pose a major challenge to international relations in the 21st century.

Nuclear Proliferation

Considerable attention has been paid to the theoretical aspects of nuclear proliferation.[9] The question that has been asked is whether nuclear proliferation refers to a single decision to acquire a nuclear weapon or is it part of a process that may stretch over a period of several years or even decades, consequently leading to the fact that no one identifiable decision can be located The proliferation puzzle, thus, has embraced an increasingly complex array of variables (Davis and Frankel, 1993; Meyer, 1984; Lavoy, 1995; Ogilive-White, 1996). Much of the literature endorses the proposition derived from political realism, which asserts that in an anarchic international environment, states will seek nuclear weapons to enhance their security. Insights from other theoretical propositions have become more commonplace in recent years. This has led to the following questions:

- What is the appropriate 'level of analysis' in studying nuclear proliferation?

- Should the focus be on the individual?
- Should the focus be on the organisations?
- Should the focus be on the cultural groups?
- Should the focus be on the state, the international system or some combination of both?

Another issue that has always been debated but is yet to be explained is the 'non-use' of nuclear weapons since 1945. This debate started very early in the nuclear calendar. Bernard Bordie argued that nuclear weapons were useful in their non-use (Colin Gray 1996, Bordie 1946). However, the main explanation of their non-use has centred on the notion of nuclear deterrence; states have been deterred from using nuclear weapons because of the concerns of retaliation in kind by adversaries. Motivations to acquire nuclear weapons, the technological determinism, the complexities of actions of sub-state, or transnational actors, the issues of nuclear smuggling, nuclear terrorism, nuclear capabilities, and intentions like South Africa declaring on March 24, 1993, that it had six nuclear weapons but had dismantled them prior to its signing the nuclear Non-Proliferation Treaty (NPT), will for long focus on the challenges that international relations will face in the 21st century.

Post Cold War Humanitarian Intervention
Humanitarian intervention poses the toughest challenge and test for an international society built on the principles of sovereignty, non-intervention and non-use of force. The society of states has committed itself in the post-holocaust world to a 'human rights culture', which outlaws genocide and mass killing. However, these humanitarian principles can, and do, conflict with those of sovereignty

and non-intervention. Sovereign states are expected to act as guardians of their 'citizens' security, but what happens when states behave like gangsters towards their own people, treating sovereignty as a licence to kill their own people. Should 'tyrannical states' be recognised as legitimate members of the international society and be accorded the protection afforded by the 'non-intervention principle'? Or should such states forfeit their sovereign rights and be exposed to legitimate intervention by international society? Related to this is the issue: what responsibilities do other states have to enforce global human rights norms against governments that massively violated them? Armed humanitarian intervention was not a legitimate practice during the Cold War period. There was a significant shift of attitude on this question during the 1990s, especially within liberal democratic states, which led to the pressing new humanitarian claims within international society. In a speech in the General Assembly of the United Nations in September 1999, it was declared that there was a "developing international norm" to forcibly protect civilians who were at risk of genocide and large scale killing. The character of this new liberal interventionism, its moral limitations and its likely evolution in a post 9/11 world are central questions that will emerge as main challenges to international relations in the 21st century. Having enumerated the challenges that the 21st century international relations face towards comprehensive security, one can address the issues related to the developments in national security and human rights in international affairs

Developments in National Security Policy-Making

Global Overview

Security as a metaphor covers a vast domain and lies beyond the paradigm attributes to be confined to any single discipline or methodology to be incorporated to find solutions, define policies, create public policy orientations or come to a consensus for accepting a general theory applicable to all issues of security. Conceptualisation of security is, thus, beyond the realm of any single discipline as it covers the very foundation of a nation-state, on the one hand, and the welfare, survival and continuation of the life of a human being, on the other. Therefore, the approach to conceptualise security has to be ensconced in an interdisciplinary approach in a multidisciplinary format. If one could compress the entire evolution of the world into a 24-hour time span, the human being would appear on planet Earth only during the last few seconds of this evolutionary period, and within this period, man has become the greatest threat to himself.

The focus of security will shift radically from the safety and sovereignty of the nation-state to the much more complex human security, cutting across international borders, covering the hitherto "non-traditional " security issues, affecting the very existence of individual human beings and requiring the securitisation of the economy, ecology, environment, pollution, energy and the rights of the unborn.

However, with all the global changes in geo-economics, and the possible environmental impact due to climate change, etc., the world, as of today, is still working on a model whose unit of analysis is the "nation-state" and whose security is not merely determined by the totality of securitisation of the human being. The military as an organisation has, as in the past, and, in the foreceable future will continue to, play a major role in maintaining the sovereignty and territorial integrity of the nation-state. The ability to enhance the vitality of a nation-state by securitising the non-traditional security issues having a direct relationship with human security will be the new challenge. Therefore, the nation-state as an autonomous actor within the global context, having the ability to strategise good governance, profitable international relations through trade and commerce, eradication of inequality within the population, maintain inclusiveness, social welfare related to health, education and employment and capacity to provide security against external threats, will become the major actor in the new global international order. Hence, the role of the military will continue to be important as a coercive force to be used against external threats and internal security risks. Conceptualising security in the present context has to be deliberately Indo-centric and it will be essential to understand the context in which Indian security has to be empowered.

Contextualising National Interest

With 202 nation-states on the roster of the United Nations, loss of bipolarity due to the demise of the former Soviet Union, proliferation of nuclear technology and weaponisation of nuclear technology creating multi-node nuclear weapon state actors, plus the complexities of globalisation whose darker side is the evolution of international terrorism, has made the study of security far more complex than what we have known or postulated even in the Cold War period. The armed forces as an organisation will become even more significant for the nation-states to be used to contain internal security problems apart from maintaining the integrity of the nation-state from external aggression or project power beyond territorial limits.

This entails the nation-states to rationalise the purpose of their national power of which one component is the organisation called the armed forces. Hence, we observe that since the 1630s, the role of national interest and defining of national interest become important to conduct the business of the present nation-state militarily, socially, politically, economically and diplomatically.

The presentation here is to facilitate the readers on the track of thinking about the concepts of theory used in conjunction with methods and methodologies in the complex mosaic of the use of force, international relations, diplomacy and internal compulsions of nation-states which have to come to grips with the crisis of identity, centre-state relationship, religion, political ideologies and diverse range of ethnic as well as multi-racial problems. All the answers to the above dilemma confronting the political elites and the managers of government lie in how each nation-state rationalises its "national interest". Secondly, national interest does not, and cannot, change with every change of government, be it a nation-state which is developed, developing or underdeveloped.

History of The Idea of National Interest

In *The Idea of National Interest* (1934), Charles Beard traced the history of the concept of 'national interest' to the 16th and 17th centuries,[10] when modern nation-states began to crystallise. Unsurprisingly, the rise of the nation-state and the use of the term occurred at the same time. Beard found that after the development of the nation-state and the appearance of nationalist sentiments, older terms – the 'will of the prince' and *'raison d'état'* – lost their ability to mobilise the public will. They were, therefore, replaced by references to 'national interests' and 'vital interests'. Other terms[11] used for their mobilising capacity include 'national honor', 'public interest' and 'general will'.[12] This followed the development of the idea of 'nation'[13] (Armstrong, 1982 and Smith, 1989).

The early history of 'national interest',[14] according to Joseph Frankel, cannot be traced back much further than the 16th century. Earlier societies that were in contact with one another often developed notions of self-interest based upon language, a common political identity, survival, power and wealth, but conceived these notions "within specific bargaining terms or conflict situations rather than in general terms".[15] Frankel writes that the concept could not be articulated in ancient Greece because of the blurring of distinctions between political and cultural communities, and the absence of clear-cut political boundaries. Conceptions of common interests were restricted to the boundaries of individual city-states, in a manner analogous to that of the Renaissance Italians. During the Persian Wars, these conceptions gave way to pan-Hellenic ideas and the more inclusive sentiment of a Hellenic cultural community. The Roman Empire accentuated the shift from national to catholic (i.e. universal) consciousness. Frankel observes that in the Middle Ages, the nature of relations between individual political units and the Roman Empire and the confusion between politics and metaphysics offered no scope for the evolution of the idea of "national interest".[16] In other words, the 'empire' superseded the 'nation' as a form of political organisation.

Before the French Revolution, the term 'nation' referred to a racial or linguistic group. Political authority was largely centralised, exclusively so in the domain of external relations; according to E.H. Carr, international relations primarily comprised relations between royal families. The narrowness of this domestic conception was matched by a mercantilist policy in external affairs. Such a policy was intended to expand the power and wealth of the state, personified by the ruler, and controlled by a small circle of governing elites. For these elites, wealth accumulation occurred as a result of the exploitation of peasants and serfs. In the post-Renaissance period, wealth accumulation also occurred as a result of trade and colonial wars. In this period, mercantilism "identified the interest of the nation with the interest of its rulers".[17]

The doctrine of *raison d'état* is a predecessor to 'national interest'. *Raison d'état* derives from Machiavelli's writings on statecraft and has its roots, according to Meinecke, in "the personal power-drive of the rulers" and "the need of the subject people, which allows itself to be governed because it receives compensations" in exchange.[18] Machiavelli argued that the overriding imperative for the ruler was the survival of the state, threats to which had to be overcome by any means necessary. The prince "must be prepared not to be virtuous, and … must not flinch from being blamed for vices which are necessary for safeguarding the state. … He should not deviate from what is good, if that is possible, but he should know how to do evil, if that is necessary".[19]

Beginning in the 15th century, and with increasing momentum in the 17th and 18th centuries, secularism and political economy began to gain in prominence at the expense of theology. This displacement from a spiritual to a material concern was matched by a corresponding change in the meaning of the word 'interest', which "shrank to an economic conception in writings and negotiations involving policy, statecraft and social affairs generally".[20] Interest referred to "outward realities such as material, plant and equipment, or aggregations of plants and equipments". It also referred to "the owners of such tangibles, as, for example, when we speak of utility interests, railroad interests, and aviation interests". The national interest, accordingly, is often regarded as "a mere aggregation of particular interests, or … the most active and dominant interests, even though they may be in the minority – considered either as the proportion of persons or corporations involved or as the proportion of capital measured by pecuniary standards",[21] Thus, for Beard, when the national interest is being considered, it is really the interests of the owners of property that are being considered. Furthermore, there is no objective 'thing' called the national interest because interests cannot be divorced from (subjective) human motives and concerns:

As far as policy is concerned, interest inheres in human beings as a motive or force of attention, affection and action… Those who merely discuss policy likewise bring their interests to bear, consciously or unconsciously, and their interests, both intellectual and economic (salary, wages or income), are affiliated with some form of ownership or opposition to the present relations or operations of ownership.[22]

The subjectivism of the term leads to the "intellectual impossibility of isolating and defining interests in absolute terms".[23] However, underpinning the whole edifice of national interest is the assumption that a given political community has common interests in distinction to the common interests of other political communities. Rousseau described the political expression of these common interests as the "general will". He suggested that there were times when the multiplicity of individual interests would be subordinated to a collective interest that is applied to all members. It is only this general will that "can direct the powers of the state in such a way that the purpose for which it has been instituted, which is the good of all, will be achieved. For, if the establishment of societies had been made necessary by the antagonism that exists between particular interests, it has been made possible by the conformity that exists between these same interests".[24]

For Rousseau, the common interests of societies constitute the basis of decision-making and policy. These interests are the cohesive glue that binds a society together and prevents it from fragmenting. The bond of society is what there is in common between these different interests, and if there were not some point in which all interests were identical, no society could exist. The bond of society is that identity of interests which all feel who compose it. In the absence of such an identity, no society would be possible. Now, it is solely on the basis of this common interest that society must be governed.[25]

Once the French Revolution had swept aside the doctrine of the 'divine right of kings', the state came to be seen as the instrument of the nation. The sovereign no longer personified the state and its interests. Beard found that claims made in the name of 'the will of the prince' lost their validity. As popular forces gained greater access to civil and political rights, the aim of national policy began to be understood as the pursuit of the interests of all members of the nation. However, the underlying assumption – that these interests existed in distinction to the interests of other political communities – continued. Governments had come under serious pressure for better wages and working conditions in the late 19th century. The Russian Revolution meant that these demands had to be taken seriously early in the 20th century. These economic interests, and the government policies that were designed to pursue them, would be asserted against the interests and policies of other governments. While this gave workers "an intimate practical interest in the policy and power of the nation", it also necessitated "the loyalty of the masses to a nation which had become the instrument of their collective interests and ambitions".[26]

Rosenau argued that the public's stake in international relations increased after World War II and with the danger of total war.[27] He suggested that 'national interest' could be used in two distinct senses – one for political analysis and another for political action. As an analytic tool, it is employed to describe, explain or evaluate the sources or the adequacy of a nation's foreign policy. As an instrument of political action, it serves as a means of justifying, denouncing or proposing policies. Both usages confine the intended meaning to what is best for a national society. Beyond these general considerations, however, the two uses of the concept have little in common.[28]

In practical terms, these distinctions are not particularly useful because there is no way to tell which of these two senses is being employed. Given the blurred distinction between the two uses, the concept is cloaked in so much ambiguity as to be unworkable. Frankel suggested another set of classifications – aspirational, operational and explanatory-polemical. At the aspirational level, national interest refers to "the vision of the good life, to some ideal set of goals which the state would like to realise if this were possible". At the operational level, "national interest refers to the sum total of interests and objectives actually pursued".[29] Frankel suggests that aspirational interests are long-term interests that are embedded in history and ideology, and invoked by a political opposition that is unrestrained by the burdens of day-to-day governance. By contrast, operational interests are short-term interests that are the primary concerns of the government and/or party in power. They arise from considerations of expediency or necessity and are used in a descriptive rather than normative form. They are "generally translated into policies which are based upon the assessment of their prospects of success".[30] At the explanatory-polemical level, the concept of national interest "is used to explain, evaluate, rationalize or criticize foreign policy. Its main role is to 'prove' oneself right and one's opponents wrong and the arguments are used for this purpose rather than for describing or prescribing".[31]

There are several problems with these classifications. For one, there is considerable overlap between the first two categories and the third. For another, the aspirational level can be utopian, often deliberately so, and unmeasurable as well. Furthermore, while the operational level describes the interests and policies actually pursued, it is thrown into confusion at the explanatory-polemical level, where a plethora of assertions and counter-assertions are to be found.

So imprecise is the term that Aaron[32] abandoned the attempt to define it, regarding it as a meaningless, vague formula or a pseudo-theory. He concluded that the national interests pursued by individual states are diverse and not at all permanent. They vary according to context and there is no general agreement even within the state about their nature.

Conceptualising National Interest

In modern political life, "national interest" has become a common term among politicians and political scientists. In nearly every discussion about changing foreign policy, national interests are treated as accepted facts to support scholars or politicians when they present opinions. But there is no accepted common standard or definition of the concept of national interest, so the understanding of the role or meaning of national interest is totally different from one user of the term to another. This makes it nearly impossible to reach a consensus when debating foreign policy. In practice, such superficial discussion is meaningless for policy-making. A debate without a common definition of national interest can never achieve a meaningful outcome. This type of debate does not help policy-makers at all in judging which recommended policy serves national interests better. In theory, such a discussion is not scientific because it is not based on a common definition of the term or a common understanding of the concept. It is like a blind person touching a part of an elephant and describing the animal based on the sense of touch only, but without any concept of what a whole elephant looks like.

Persons in foreign affairs circles and others dealing with international relations theory must have a similar concept of national interest when discussing our country's foreign policy. It is necessary to establish common standards for defining national interests. Without common standards, it will be impossible to make the study of foreign policy scientific; it will also be difficult to have meaningful discussions on foreign policy. For instance, there are people who regard 16 liang (similar to ounces) as 1 jin (similar to pounds); others regard 10 liang as 1 jin; there are even people who regard 9 liang as 1 jin. If their counts of liang are the same, they can never reach an agreement on the weight of any given object using the concept of jin. If their concepts of liang are different, they will not have the same outcome when weighing objects, in addition they may also confuse the concepts of heavy and light.

Confused Concepts of National Interest
Let me illustrate with China as an example. National interest does not have a class nature In the Chinese language, the concept of "national interest" has two meanings. One is national interest in the context of international politics, meaning the interests of a nation-state in the global arena. This concept must be contrasted with group interests, international interests or global interests. The other is

state interest or interests of the state as the highest level in domestic politics, meaning governmental interest or a government that represents the people's interest. Interests of the state are more important than local interests, collective interests or individual interests. In 1954, Chairman Mao, at an extended meeting of the Chinese Communist Party Politburo, said "Our policy toward farmers is not like the Soviets', but it is one that takes care of both the interests of farmers and the interests of the state."[33] The national interest that Mao Zedong was talking about is in the category of domestic politics. In 1989, when Deng Xiaoping met with the Thai Prime Minister, he said, "China wants to maintain its own national interest, sovereignty and territorial integrity. China also believes that a socialist country cannot violate other countries' interests, sovereignty or territory."[34] The national interest that Deng Xiaoping was talking about here meant national interest in the context of international politics. Premier Zhou Enlai said in 1949: "When no war or violation takes place, national interests need to be protected domestically and internationally. In the international arena, diplomacy has become frontline work."[35]

Because of the dual meaning of "national interest" in the Chinese language, some scholars have confused national interest with the interest of the state. They have, therefore, misunderstood the meaning of the concept of national interest in the context of international politics. Lenin said the state is an instrument of the ruling class in domestic politics. State organisations are that instrument. Because the ruling class controls the state, its interest and that of the ruling class coincide. A state's interest is often contrary to groups other than the ruling class; therefore, national interests in terms of domestic politics do have a class nature.

However, a state in international politics represents a political entity that consists of four major elements: population, territory, government and international recognition. This state is sometimes called a country. After the modern nation-state was formed, a country has also been called a nation. This is why the UN is called the United Nations. The term "nation" is a political concept for all people of a country. Its focus is national but certainly not class-based. The national interest in international politics includes the interests of the whole nation-state. And both the ruler and the ruled share those interests.

Logically, it is paradoxical to say that the ruling class represents national interests. The state in the context of domestic politics is a tool of the ruling class. That tool always reflects the user's will, not vice versa. In other words, it is the state that represents the ruler's interest not the ruler who represents the state's interest. A nation in international politics is not a ruling tool; it is a political group of people. Therefore, it definitely represents the interests of the entire group. It cannot represent the interests of only a part of the people within the group. Thus, national interests are represented by a government but not by a class. By equating national interest with ruling class interest, the differences between a nation and a political regime have been blurred. Ruling class interests are not national interests but only interests of a regime in power. In fact, because national interests differ from ruling class interests, a country's government sometimes sacrifices the national interests to maintain ruling class interests.

In a country that integrates religion and politics, as in some Islamic countries in the Middle East, national interests often overlap religious interests. In modern democratic countries like America and the Western European countries, it is the political party, not the religious organisation, which is at the helm of the state. In some countries where there is no party in control, national interests often overlap with the key political leader's individual interests. In Russia, after the disintegration of the Soviet Union, for example, the key political leader, Boris Yeltsin, did not rely on his political party for governing but on his charisma. These are all indisputable facts. However, these phenomena only occur under certain historical conditions, therefore, we cannot draw a universal conclusion that national interests have a religious nature, a political party nature or an individual nature. Likewise, the overlap of national interests with ruling class interests is also conditional.

Definition of National Interest

What exactly is national interest? Napoleon had said that he was acting in the interest of France when he initiated his campaign against Russia, and later when he launched his desperate battle at Waterloo. Adolf Hitler justified his expansionist policies, including annexation of Austria and break-up of Czechoslovakia, in the name of Germany's national interest. "Friendly socialist" governments were installed in Poland and other East European countries by Stalin in the name of the Soviet Union's national interest. President Bush was acting in America's national interest when he led the war against Iraq on the question of Kuwait's annexation by Iraq. Benazir Bhutto thought that it was in Pakistan's national interest to destabilise the Indian state of Jammu and Kashmir.

Thus, all actions, howsoever wrong, are taken in the name of national interest. We must now try to find an acceptable definition of national interest. The idea of national interest is singularly vague. It assumes a variety of meanings in different contexts. The concept of national interest has not been objectively or scientifically defined. However, Padleford and Lincoln observe : "Concepts of national interests are centred on the core values of the society, which include the welfare of the nation, the security of its political beliefs, national way of life, territorial integrity and its self-preservation." According to Robert Osgood, national interest is a "state of affairs valued solely for its benefit to the nations." Morgenthau maintains that the main requirements of a nation-state are to protect its physical, political and cultural identity against threats from other states. But, Joseph Frankel writes about the aspirational and operational and aspects of national interest. Aspirational (what one expects) aspects include the state's vision of a good life and an ideal set of goals to be realised. Put into operation, national interest refers to the sum total of its interests and policies actually pursued.

Because the label "national interest" is so broad, it is like pinpricks in a black paper with a bright light behind it, shining on a wall. If you had 1,000 pinpricks, then you would have constellations of interests out there.

Therefore, the government tries to narrow the definition of "national interest" to:

- Defence.
- National security.
- Economy.
- Inter-state and foreign commerce.
- Foreign relations.
- And the state of general national affairs.

A good examples that can be set in concrete with national interest is, for instance, a federal energy policy. Since 'energy' is at the root of just about every issue, from transportation, national defence, commerce and foreign relations, not to mention national security, etc. and since it is strategic in nature, energy is a 'national interest'.

The reason why it is so hard to nail down is that national interest is so varied and extends into so many corners of our daily lives—it is sometimes hard to define only one area unless it is a glaring one. Another area would be defence. The defence of this nation requires a standing military made up of several branches. Therefore, it is in our national interest to have a strong and capable military.

Formulating National Interest

This brings us to the question: how is national interest formulated?

National interest and the nation-state are not twins. Did national interests emerge along with the interests of human beings? The answer is no. The reason is simple. If there is no state, then there is no national interest. Interest is a social concept. Its subject is, of course, human beings with a social nature. For various reasons, human beings are classified into various types and groups. Thus, interests also vary: individual interests, family interests, children's interests, women's interests, class interests, party interests, social interests, government interests, etc.

A nation is the most basic human group or actor in international politics; therefore, it is the most important social entity of interests in the global context. As a political unit, states were formed when mankind reached a certain stage of development. Therefore, the concept of national interest did not exist before the formation of states. Did the concept of national interest emerge with the state? The answer is still in the negative. This is because national interest is largely defined as the interest of the modern nation-state. But the concept of the modern nation-state emerged relatively late in human history. Therefore, it is impossible that national interest emerged with the early formation of states. It took as many as thousands of years for some states to develop into modern nation-states.

In the 1950s, China had economic relations with only 40 or so countries. China's overseas economic interests were, therefore, limited to trade with these countries. By the beginning of the 1980s, China had established economic and trade relations with 178 countries and regions; obviously, the scope of its economic interest had expanded.Along with the continuous implementation of the open door policy, the scope of China's overseas national interest will naturally expand even further. After the disintegration of the Soviet Union, Russia's domestic politics became chaotic. China believes that Russia's domestic political stability is important to China's interests. Therefore, China developed policies to support Yeltsin in stabilising domestic politics. After the Sino-Russian foreign ministers talks in 1992, Foreign Minister Qian Qichen addressed journalists. He said: "Central Asian countries have close ties with Russia in every aspect and, at the same time, are members of the Commonwealth of Independent States. China and Russia share a common interest in keeping Central Asia stable and economically prosperous."

Utility of National Interest

If the definition of national interest can be warped in so many ways, what good is the concept? It's only as good as your ability to perceive reality accurately, a gift granted to few. For the rest of us, to get an accurate fix on national interest, it would be necessary to travel into the future in a time machine to see how things worked out under a given policy. The real national interest is sometimes knowable only many years after the fact. Second- and third-order effects of a policy are often wildly unpredictable. In the mid-1960s, Vietnam seemed to most Americans to be a national interest; a decade later, few thought it had been one. The victorious Communists in Vietnam, having impoverished their country, now seek to enter the capitalistic world market economy. Funny how things work out. The utility of national interest is not in any formula that can untangle complex issues. National interest is useful in training the decision-maker to ask a series of questions, such as: How are current developments affecting my nation's power? Are hostile forces able to harm my vital interests? Do I have enough power to protect my vital interests? Which of my interests is secondary? How much of my power am I willing to use to defend them? What kind of deals can I get in compromises over secondary interests? The net impact of these questions is to restrain impetuous types from embarking on crusades.

Morgenthau's argument is that the world would be a much better place if all statesmen would consistently ask such questions, for that would induce a sense of limit and caution into their strategies that might otherwise be lacking. For those who simply will not keep their national interests defined tightly and close to home but instead are intent on expanding their power (imperialism), Morgenthau's approach is also useful. The statesman is constantly scanning the horizon to detect the growth of hostile power centres, and if they seem likely to impinge on his national interests, he formulates strategies to safeguard them, each step grounded on adequate power. The national interest approach is terribly old-fashioned and some thinkers argue it has been, or must be, superseded by "world interest" or "world order" approaches, which go beyond the inherent selfishness of national interest. Empirically, however, one would still find national interest a better predictor of state strategy than world order. In a crisis, when it comes to putting their troops in harm's way, statesmen still ask themselves, "What is my nation's interest in all this?" It is still not a bad question.

PART 2

THEORETICAL MOORINGS OF INDIA'S FOREIGN POLICY: NEHRU TO MODI

Neither Nehru nor Narendra Modi has been associated with an institutionalised doctrinal approach to foreign policy-making. One can, however, see the use of the term Gujral Doctrine[36] or newfound truncated version called Manmohan Singh Doctrine.[37] The theoretical moorings of India's foreign policy-making become more disjointed when one takes into account the joke that circulated amongst the graduate students pursuing their doctoral work towards the end of the last century. It stated, "Gandhiji was convinced that there were moral solutions to political problems, Nehru considered pursuing idealism as a solution to all political problems, Indira Gandhi thought that there were political solutions to moral problems, and Rajiv Gandhi was convinced that technology could solve all problems – political and moral."

However, scholars from the national and international arenas must recognise on a serious note that attention to India's foreign policy-making has attracted major intellectual inputs. The most preferred way of approaching the 70 years of India's independent history will be to create time capsule modules and then observe how each section of the historical periods contributed towards the identification of the theoretical moorings of India's foreign policy-making.

In 2017, India would be celebrating the 70th year of independence and witnessing the implications of foreign and national security perspectives operating from within the complex mosaic of International Relations (IR) in the post World War II period which has seen the end of the classical bipolarity and the Cold War, emergence of globalisation and the rise of terrorism. The emerging world order is characterised by economic and political interdependence and has virtually made redundant the traditional understanding of IR in its functional modality.[38] Hence, coverage of the past 70 years has to be divided into two neat parts. First, the Nehruvian period, and the second, the post Nehruvian period till date with the emergence of Narendra Modi who dawned on the scene just a little more than two years ago, in 2014.

It is, indeed, a daunting task to encapsulate the understanding of India's rise to a global status of power, both militarily and economically, within the ultra-short confines of the space of this article – an issue area on which volumes have been written with vigorous intellectual inputs from scholars from all over the world. It will be prudent to observe that the rise of the economic and political power of India and China have been spectacular, despite India's feeble foreign policy.[39]

However, India has not undertaken any step in the past 70 years to institutionalise the national security policy-making process, nor has it defined the incorporation of stakeholders and their role. Like the foreign policy-makers are insulated from outside influence, the makers and deliberators of national security policy decisions remain highly individualistic, hostage to those who hold key positions such as National Security Adviser (NSA) and have the ears of the Prime Minister. There are hardly any publicly accepted inputs from the non-partisan strategic planners or experts belonging to the think-tanks, academia or public intellectuals[40] by the government in the real sense. This, when compounded with the lack of institutionalised mechanisms to cull out coherent foreign policy, has resulted in a lethal combination of personal perceptions based on strong opinions being resorted to, both by the political elites and the bureaucracy, to frame the foreign policy agenda, goals and objectives by successive governments that held constitutional powers to administer India rather than govern it.

Dividing the Timeframe of Indian Democracy

Historically, at a macro level, two timeframes can be constructed to study the trends and making of Indian foreign policy. We have to understand the political, social and economic objectives pursued by the heads of the government during the two timeframes to understand the theoretical moorings of India's foreign policy making/ compulsions. They are:

1. First Timeframe from 1947 to 1964: The Nehru Era

2. Second Timeframe – Post 1964: India in World Affairs

First Timeframe 1947-64: The Nehru Era

The Nehru Era: The first timeframe (1947 to 1964) was totally dominated singularly by Nehru as the first Prime Minister. He never divested himself of the portfolio of Foreign Minister nor did he allow any of his Cabinet colleagues or celebrated friends who belonged to the scientific world or those who were internationally acclaimed intellectuals or scholars belonging to the academia to provide any alternative theoretical paradigm for foreign policy-making in India. One of the most interesting anecdotes which demonstrates Nehru's total monopoly over foreign policy matters, relates to Bhabha and Nehru. When the former tried to advise him on the nuclear issue, Nehru just told him, "You look after physics and leave the politics to me". And earlier, Nehru's non-action on the famous letter written to him by Sardar Patel[41] about the need to reassess India's assessment about China and the assured rise of China in the very near future as a potential adversary to India needs to be recorded. Yet he permitted Krishna Menon to have his way on matters strategic and military which resulted in a military debacle for India in 1962 – the effect of which still haunts the Indian strategic psyche and in which Nehru lost face, and which ultimately saw the end of his political leadership.

However, it will be myopic to underscore the complexity of Nehru's mind or underscore his world view, which began evolving early and was noticeable in his Brussels speech in 1927—idealistic and utopian in nature, influenced by Wendel Wilkie's notion of "One World". The post-war period and his taking over as the first Prime Minister of India made him realise the nature of power of the superpowers, the imperfections inherent in the international state system, and the shortcomings of the UN. His visit to the Soviet Union impressed him immensely to become a socialist at heart but his Western upbringing and liberal democratic moorings made him acutely aware of the positivity of the market economy, the need to establish privatisation of production of consumer goods and, hence, create an internal world view rooted in democratic ideals. Michael Breecher, as his political biographer, wrote, "Nehru in the Parliament was the leader of the ruling party and, at the same, time acted as the leader of the opposition". Breecher, later on, in his book *Krishna Menon's View of World* based on 14 interviews of Krishna Menon came out with a theoretical model of foreign policy-making in India and attributed Nehru's perceptions of the world order as a direct product of his Western educations and his idealism of a just society, which was impractical to be institutionalised in the modern nation-state system, This theoretical model famously known as the Breecher-Stein-Steinburg model was used by Professor Janice Gross Stein in the early Sixties of the last century for her doctoral thesis to undertake a content analysis of Nehru's speeches for his perceptions and world view. This study was perhaps the most unparadigmic approach in international relations theory to the foreign policy-making of a political leader of the largest democracy in the world.

It will be essential to record the tumultuous time in which Nehru lived and saw the unfolding of the history of conflict and war at the global level. He saw the decimation of Germany and Japan, and the rise of the US and the Soviet Union as superpowers. He understood well that there was "no asymmetry" of power at the levels amongst the two superpowers and his scientific temper made him understand that the diktat of the nuclear weapons states mattered empirically and that they would only respond to power. He knew only too well that India had to keep its nuclear options open at all times. Nehru was a humanist in heart and mind and was passionate to further the cause of human rights, speak about apartheid in the UN, and work to make nations follow international law. He singularly made an impact globally at the historic Bandung Conference in 1955, spoke in universities abroad and in India too, not only about his views on foreign policy but on the universalism to be perpetuated through the portals of higher education, and recorded his concept of peace at the UN General Assembly as early as in 1954.

While the reality of the Cold War in a bipolar war did not go unnoticed by Nehru, his perceptions and total intellectual rejection of the correlation of war with the balance of power paradigm made him search for a model of world governance in which wars and occurrence of war could be made redundant. He wanted to speak to, and be heard by, the superpowers and not address at them merely through the UN. He considered that if the newly emerged and lesser powers of the world could be united through the adoption of common principles, acting through a common forum, and if India could be kept out of the military alliance system created by the two superpowers, then there would be hope to reduce, and ultimately eradicate, the dangers of a global nuclear war. He went on to draft the Panchsheel, the five principles of peaceful coexistence and later, gave shape to the Non-Alignment Movement (NAM) which immediately saw takers found amongst a number of nation-states which had particularly fought for freedom during the colonial era. Nehru's world view attempted to synergise a set of nation-states that would in principle remain away from being entangled by the superpowers. In essence, it was the idealistic approach attempted by Nehru to perpetuate global peace, justice and equity amongst nation-states, irrespective of their military or technological capabilities. He not only believed in the approach to world politics through diplomacy and consensus but also in the futility of creating military power even for national security perspectives. He had a life-long suspicion of the "man on horseback" and did everything in the context of the Indian armed forces and forced the organisation to be relegated to a non-entity in the formative stage of India's development. He was, thus, singularly responsible for the non-development of a strategic culture envisaging the use of military force to achieve any political goal in post-independent India – a trend whose germination he permitted all through his 17 years as the Prime Minister of India. His celebrated Defence Minister Krishna Menon was never a popular figure amongst the Service Chiefs. On one occasion, when a very distinguished Service Chief projected that India needed 150 divisions to safeguard India from external threats, Menon told him that he would solve the entire border problem in 150 words. With the military debacle in 1962, the romantic myth of assured national security through diplomacy collapsed, Nehru was shattered psychologically, losing political credibility, and the rest is history which set into motion the restructuring, reassessments, modernisation and role of the Indian Army.

Theoretical Moorings of Nehruvian Foreign Policy-Making: With the compressed narrative of the Nehru era given above, a short and concise attempt can be made to understand the theoretical moorings of Indian foreign policy-making under Nehru. Nehru was not only critical of, but never accepted, the *Machtpolitik* i.e. the politics of the use of power. He was a realist to the core, as can be seen in his essays in

Young India on "Defence of India" way back in 1931. A P Rana observes, "One is struck by their realist logic, well before realism as statecraft (in the late 1930s) cut into the earlier climate of Idealism and much before Realism as an international theoretical formulation of that statecraft got enunciated."[42] Nehru was also a product of the high idealism of the "Indian Renaissance" of the 19th and early 20th centuries. Gandhi's influence on Nehru was profound and his total participation in the freedom movement for independence could be seen "as a part of the larger movement for the regeneration of India's civilization".[43] As a realist, Nehru sought to respond to the bipolar world by using the policy of non-alignment to achieve strategic autonomy for India. He was the first to recognise the importance of the need to include the centrality of Asia in his foreign policy formulation and pursue a relentless proactive posture on issues of the global order.[44] As a realist, his theoretical moorings of foreign policy-making allowed him to attempt, and be successful, between national security goals and the normative system level concerns in world affair. This resulted in his success to contain bipolarity, relationship independence in foreign policy-making, and strategically isolate Pakistan and China.[45] Again, as a realist, and not succumbing to idealism, Nehru's disenchantment with the UN on the Kashmir issue led to his giving a mid-course correction by not taking the Sino-Indian border issue, the Goa occupation and the whole range of river waters involving the neighbouring countries to any international organisation for any type of arbitration. Nehru kept India away from any participation in any international border disputes, refrained from taking sides with China and its multiple disputes with Japan in Korea, Indo-China or elsewhere.[46] It is, thus, clear that the theoretical moorings of India's foreign policy-making were deeply ensconced in the world vision that Nehru had and, more interestingly, his conceptualisation of Realism, Liberalism and Internationalism was an outcome of his deeper understanding of world affairs and his life, which not only witnessed the two World Wars but also his personal participation in the Indian freedom struggle with the great Mahatma on his side, spiritually, ideologically and intellectually, as well as his responsibility for the debacle of the India-China War in 1962.

Second Timeframe – Post 1964: India in World Affairs

Post 1964: India in World Affairs: After Nehru, India has seen 15 Indian Prime Ministers, with Gulzari Lal Nanda being acting Prime Minister twice. This post-independence period spanned 52 years filled with more complexities in international relations than what existed during Nehru's time. While Nehru could display a world vision and influence the course of the debate in respect of global governance, it was not possible for those who followed Nehru to acquire the same status, or display the idealism, liberalism and internationalism that Nehru did. The superpowers' arms race, technology to create massive stockpiles of nuclear weapons and other forms of weapons of mass destruction, incremental increase in the Cold War divide, non-alignment reduced to a forum rather than as a movement for the non-nuclear states to remain away from alliance politics,[47] rise of China as a major world power, economically and militarily, nuclear proliferation and emergence of new nuclear capable nation-states, balkanisation of the Soviet Union, bipolarity giving way to multipolarity, information revolution, globalisation and economic interdependence, emergence of international terrorism, border wars, climate change, energy security and a whole range of issues related to the non-strategic dimensions covering the ecology, environment, pollution, energy and the rights of the unborn became major issues to be addressed by all nation-states, rich or poor, developed or underdeveloped, democratic or authoritarian, and became part of the complex mosaic within which the Indian political leadership had to operate.

Of the 202 countries that were members of the UN, only 22 were given the status of fully developed nation-states while all the others were classified as developing, underdeveloped and less developed states. Strategic calculations and projection of power by all nation-states took a new dimension to enunciate their individual national security policies, and the notion that defence policy could be pursued through diplomacy became invalid. The world faced newer challenges in the form of fundamentalist movements, international piracy and effects of the narco trade and water security issues between neighbouring nation-states. China's aggressive posture to not only assert itself as a major power, next to the US, but its strategy to encircle India by economic and strategic agglomerations all through the past 52 years has become an acute factor for consideration by the Indian political leadership today.

In these past 52 years, the Indian political leadership significantly contributed to raise India to a power status despite its feeble foreign policy-making[48] architecture. As all the abovementioned issues form a part of foreign policy deliberations, one can easily see that amongst the 14 Prime Ministers who held office during the period mentioned, five undertook specific actions before Modi dawned on the scene as a possible game changer in 2014. These issues covered during this period relate to bilateral security arrangements called "Treaty of Friendship", nationalisation of banks, wars with Pakistan, liberation of Bangladesh, liberalisation of the economy, conduct of the nuclear test in 1998, and signing of the Indo-US Strategic Partnership. Apart from all this listing, the successive Prime Ministers in office also faced the perennial problems with Pakistan and China, and bilateral relationship problems with the South Asian Association for Regional Cooperation (SAARC) countries, plus involvement in Afghanistan. All these issues had to be tackled with a horribly understaffed Ministry of External Affairs (MEA) which till date does not have the ability to undertake any long range policy studies to aid the government adequately.[49] Modi's taking over as Prime Minister may turn out to be a possible game changer in the approach to foreign affairs in India. However, it is too early to acknowledge, or feel elated about it. There is a lot of hype and the results are yet to arrive. Nonetheless, there appears to be silver lining on the horizon. It will, hence, be best now to examine the theoretical moorings of India's foreign policy-making in this second timeframe.

Theoretical Moorings of FP Making in post 1964 Period: Basrur observes, "The analysis of Indian foreign policy often tends to lack conceptual clarity and a sound theoretical base". Amitabh Acharya sounds a greater concern by stating that "international relations theory in the South Asian context is a-theoretical...." And that "the field has been hijacked by the area specialists". It is, hence, an unenviable task to find a sound basis to locate the theoretical moorings of India's foreign policy-making when a large canvas of the time span between Shastri and Modi is reviewed. The constraints of space do not allow a detailed comprehensive treatment to enable a complete overview of all issues that the fifteen Prime Ministers faced in order to formulate the foreign policy in terms of the Indian context. However, neo-realist perspectives to analyse India's external behaviour will allow us to notice the behavioural patterns and identify the noticeable changes in those patterns in which interactions can be the independent variable and structure the dependent variable,[50] and how India created strategies at the sub-continental and global levels. This is because a neo-realistic system theory provides an overall perspective and helps to identify the general pattern of behaviour in international politics at the cost of studying the details and specifics. While theories in social sciences cannot claim to be predictive or precise, neo-realism highlights tendencies and trends related to power and interest as the main motives to be pursued by any state with regard to war and peace, alliances, and the general problems of inter-state cooperation[51]. During this period of time, India faced two conceptually different types of system: the subcontinental and the global. Again, paucity of space does not allow a detailed critique of Realism versus Liberalism or how the post-positivists critically attribute the political conservatism of the realists as 'problem solving' to maintain 'status quo' by specifically evading moral and ethical questions, particularly in a democratic structure. It is important to understand that the universalism propounded by neo-realism to explain world politics may be falling short, according the criticism of the post positivists, yet neo-realism does explain a whole range of state behaviour within the power-interest matrix. As Basrur points out, "Neo-realism rejects the cloak of morality and high sounding principles that states frequently use to dress up interest-based politics". There are many issues that the neo-realist system theory fall shorts of explaining, especially the relationship between Weapons of Mass Destruction (WMD) technology and deterrence policies to avoid wars, but it certainly explains what Basrur calls "the intensity of interaction between nuclear powered states". He further makes it clear, "Intensity is a property of the system rather than of its member states. It determines the extent to which structure shapes state behaviour in a system."

All Indian Prime Ministers within the demarcated time capsule had, and will continue, to address their foreign policies at two levels. One, towards the subcontinental/regional system encompassing the states that are part of SAARC and, two, the overarching global system. Of course, Modi will have to even go beyond the traditional SAARC countries to as far as Iran on one side and the states involved in the South China Sea (SCS) imbroglio. Manmohan Singh had no SCS factor to contend with and Indira Gandhi could correlate with the former Soviet Union to cater for the sub-regional conflict and come out with a resounding political and military success by creating Bangladesh without the physical involvement of either the US or China.

Hence, the following five observations will be pertinent to make:

- The theoretical moorings of India's foreign policy-making can only be found under Nehru as the Prime Minister of India. A B Vajpayee restricted his statesmanship mainly to conflict resolution at the bilateral international relationship level between India and Pakistan.
- It was Vajpayee who theoretically gave the geopolitical reality of "one does not have any choice to choose neighbours but has the choice to choose friends". Both Nehru and Vajpayee demonstrated their preference for classical liberal realism.
- Nehru and Vajpayee have been the only two Prime Ministers who imbibed the principles of "governing to administer and not administering to govern".
- The entire post Nehru period of Indian history has been marked by practical constructivism in one form or the

other to shape India's National Interest (NI), Foreign Policy (FP) and National Security (NS). At best, they remained bilateral in nature without any global aspirations.

- Narsimha Rao concentrated on unshackling the Indian economy from the licence raj, while Vajpayee succeeded in declaring India a nuclear weapons state. However, the circumstances and the vagaries of the political environment robbed Manmohan Singh, an internationally reputed economist and Prime Minister for ten years, of the opportunity to articulate a firm theoretical mooring to his foreign policy endeavours even through the conceptual lens of economics.

As the triad of national interest, foreign policy and national security form an interrelated issue area and perspective in a modern nation-state, India in the post-independence period, has failed to create a seamless architecture to bridge the gap between the realm of ideas and the domain of public policy-making and define each of them in a way to institutionalise an organic interdependent relationship amongst the triad in the largest democracy in the world.

The present government, led by Narendra Modi, is developing a paradigm shift on foreign policy issues, which are intricately linked to national security perspectives. His outreach to the Indian Diaspora around the world, his digital connectivity with individuals cutting across the globe, his use of technology to create a hype for his persona, and his physical energy to work 24x7 have to be acknowledged even by his distractors. However, it is too early to state whether Modi's world views can be labelled as yet or whether there is a theoretical mooring to his foreign policy-making endeavours.

PART 3

THE NATIONAL SECURITY POLICY-MAKING PRISM: THE INDIAN CONTEXT

Any discussion on the national security policy-making prism has to take into consideration the following:

1. **The Historical Reality**

2. **The Indian Dilemma**

Historical Reality

India, on gaining independence in 1947, inherited many disadvantages. Despite carrying the baggage of accumulated misuse over the centuries, it did have one natural advantage of gaining a resurgent nationalism on getting independence in

1947. One should not fail to note that India had been a subject nation for centuries, without achieving the status of a nation-state or experiencing the culture of nationhood. India's diversity, its multi-cultural, multi-racial, multi-religious and multi-ethnic characteristics were greatly derided, as well as destroyed and literally shut down. India also bore the consequences of servitude and the humiliation of military defeat at the hands of invaders from outside, over centuries. Interestingly, India became subservient to its inherited partitioned geography, which created Pakistan. This aspect has led to the unending interpretation of its territorial integrity by outside powers to the extent of being internationalised by the members of international organisations. Indian history and historical traditions became bardic, mainly subaltern, remembered from time to time more romantically and emotionally in a mythological way, with the monuments created in the past by some Indian heroes being seen as historical sites and never as a source of inspiration to be carried forward in an incremental force to produce nationalism. Indians in the pre-independence period displayed a strange fixity on the battles of Panipat, or the exploits of Shivaji, Tipu Sultan, Rana Sanga or Porus—something that is hardly relevant today. These historical events have hardly served as building blocks to evolve any basis of a strategic culture in the post-independence India. Paradoxically, India has attempted a more ambitious and more modern, less medieval and less occidental nationalism.

Conceptually, the Indian political class, as leaders of the largest democracy, even at the time of independence, committed an unpardonable error in searching for the sustaining roots of Indian nationhood in alien idioms, values and norms. The acceptance of the geographical division of undivided India, agreed to by the political blunder committed by the Indian political leadership and decision-making influenced by the outgoing British Raj has, today created a crisis of identity of the nation-state's nomenclature which has remained undefined: Bharat, Hindustan or India. While the moral and psychological momentum of the freedom movement carried on till the disastrous military setback in 1962, thanks to the idealism of Nehru and illiteracy of Krishna Menon on military matters, India dissipated the high moral and practical aspects of nationalism to guide the destiny of independent India. This, coupled with the confusion created by Gandhian pacifism and compounded by the initiation of non-alignment as a foreign policy tool to address the hard realities of real politik played by the superpowers during the Cold War period and the absurdity of rewriting non-alignment as non-alignment 2.0 as late as in 2013 by a group of public intellectuals in collusion with some of the top bureaucrats responsible to craft India's strategic policies, reduced India's strategic thinking to irrelevancy by the end of the term of the last government in office in 2014.[52] Earlier, in 1990-91, Jaswant Singh had noted the stark reality of Indian thinking and assessment on matters military in the following way:

> We thought that all warfare and strategy were about individual valor and bravery; we thought our soldiers are the best in the world (yes, they are, but is that all?) We thought besides, "What does India, well meaning India, have to fear from any quarter?" To my mind, this was, in turn, both a consequence and a cause. This mentality was the consequence of the failure to evolve an Indian state, and became the cause, in turn, failing to do so even after independence. Also, the defining catalyst in the evolution of nation-states in the West, the industrial revolution, had

entirely missed India; our historical experience was, thus, altogether different. But we did not recognize that perhaps inevitably, therefore, with no inheritance of strategic thought, with our land vivisected geographically otherwise; equally, with scarce incentives for conceptualizing independently such a thought, with our political leadership either ignorant or unconcerned or both, an evolution of this irreplaceable ingredient remained limited in the extreme…That is why conclusions as those of George Tanham, widely distributed throughout the international strategic community, did not seem to greatly surprise or even pain anyone in India. Nor did it result in any other reaction, even one of correction. The implications, however, of this seeming inability of people of great antiquity and cultural resilience are grave and cannot be escaped… Wars, historians have noted, are decided by three factors: terrain, the difference of the levels of armament technology; and the character, attitude, and approach of the contending sides. The terrain is given, and technology can be improved, but the last cannot be easily remedied. And this last has been India's main deficiency and principle reason for the lack of any intelligible national strategic thought.

That India till 1995 did not have a declared defence policy but only guidelines is evident from Jaswant Singh's address entitled "What Constitutes National Security in a Changing World Order? India's Strategic Thought", published as CASI Occasional Paper Number June 06, 1998. The relevant part of the publication is appended below for the record:

For many years now, in fact, for five terms in Parliament, I have been seeking from successive governments a clear, intelligible, comprehensive and reliable enunciation of our defense policy.

I offer but two, somewhat lengthy, quotations The first, the reply of the Government when, as Chairman of a Committee of Parliament, I had asked them to explain their policy. This was in 1990-91. In April 1995, I again asked the Government to clarify their policy. The then Prime Minister, as Defence Minister, responded. I quote both statements in full without any additional comments.

In 1990, the then Defence Secretary stated during evidence:

I would submit that perhaps we have not been able to convince the honourable committee through our various notes that there is a policy. It is perhaps not defined in the manner that the committee was looking for.

He further added:

There is a document called the Operational Directives. It is a fairly comprehensive paper, which is issued from the Defence Secretary to the three Chiefs of Staff. It seeks to bring about as clearly as possible, under the given circumstances, the threat situation which has been visualised in consultation not only with the three Services but the various agencies, the Ministry of External Affairs, as necessary with the Home Ministry in consultation with the Prime Minister's Office and, finally, it is approved by the Defence Minister. We have such a document, which has been in existence for a considerable period.

We found on closer examination that the contents of this document required considerable change because of the enormous change that has taken place or is taking place not only in our near immediate vicinity but all round. We have, in the past year or so been getting the views, comments, perceptions of the three Services and have prepared a fresh document which has been very closely examined by the various concerned authorities in the Government. We found that there is a large number of areas where we were not in agreement. We set up a group of Senior Officers to sit together and come to a debated view on the basic minimum definition of what the country perceives as existing or emerging threats. That document is virtually finalised. It is now to go to the higher echelons.

Now, if you ask, is this the defence policy, I would not be able to say the answer is in the affirmative because India's defence policy, to the extent that I can venture to make a statement, from 1947 onwards, more precisely from 1950 onwards, has been basically a policy to defend our territory, our sovereignty and our freedom and no more than that. But from time to time, vis-a-vis our immediate neighbours, vis-a-vis Bangladesh at a point of time and vis-a-vis Sri Lanka more recently, the policy proceeded to grapple with the problem as it arose. Whatever kind of background we may be able to build up in consultation with various concerned authorities, I venture to submit that it may not still be of the kind that the Committee have in mind.

The policy must be clear and this should be a subject to debate. I am afraid that it may not be there for the moment. But still there is an ongoing and continuing effort on all fronts, within the Services, within our Ministry. We are interacting with the various concerned departments and organisations of the Government. We are trying to proceed very rapidly in that direction. The recent decision of the

Government to set up the National Security Council was another step in the same direction. It should not be left merely to the household of the Ministry of Defence or a few other concerned organisations to come to whatever view they think as most accurate. We have to try to expose the perceptions and the concepts to academics, to people from various walks of life, retired civil servants, retired Defence Service officers, academicians, people from the universities and parliamentarians who have been interested in the subject. So what is ultimately established as the national perception of what requires to be done, would be fairly well tested, on a broad basis.

On 16 May 1995, the Prime Minister and Minister of Defence, Shri P. V. Narasimha Rao, stated:

Mr. Speaker, Sir, I would only confine myself to a few matters, a very few matters impinging on the defence policy of the Government and I would like to take the House into confidence and explain these things to the best possible extent, to the extent I can.

Sir, the first criticism has been rather an extraordinary kind of criticism to say that we have no National Defence Policy. I would like to submit very respectfully that this is not true.

We do not have a document called India's National Defence Policy but we have got several guidelines, which are followed, strictly followed and observed, and those can be summed up as follows:

1. *To defend our national territory over land, sea and air, encompassing among others the inviolability of our land borders, island territories, offshore assets and our maritime trade routes.*

2. *To secure an internal environment whereby our nation-state is insured against any threats to its unity or progress on the basis of religion, language, ethnicity or socio-economic dissonance.*

3. *To be able to exercise a degree of influence over the nations in our immediate neighbourhood to promote harmonious relationships in tune with our national interests.*

4. *To be able to effectively contribute towards regional and international stability and to possess an effective out-of-the-country contingency capability to prevent destabilisation of the small nations in our immediate neighbourhood that could have adverse security implications for us.*

This policy is not merely [sic] rigid in the sense that it has been written down, but these are the guidelines....

I think no more explanation or elaboration is needed...."

From the above exposition, it can be clearly inferred that for the first 50 years after India's independence, the political leadership has made the utterances on defence policy not through a policy document but as guidelines produced by the bureaucracy without any inputs from the Indian intellectual community at large or various stakeholders, in a transparent way. There have only been talks but without any will to implement a robust defence policy or recording of any strategy for national security nor any attempt to define India's national interest.

Even today, there is no official enunciation of a Defence Policy of India by the government, no official document enumerating the National Security Strategy and no White Paper on Defence Strategy like those published by the US, UK, China, Australia or many other countries listed below:

- *Lebanon: The Lebanese Defensive Policy in Light of Vital Interests*
- *Bélgique: Le plan stratégique 2000-2015 à mi-parcours*
- *Japan: Defence of Japan 2014*
- *France: French White Paper 2013*
- *Spain: The National Security Strategy*
- *Finnish Security and Defence Policy 2012*
- *Strong and Secure: A Strategy for Australia's National Security 2013*
- *France: Defence and National Security 2013*
- *Norwegian Defence 2013*
- *Japan: Defence of Japan 2013*
- *Australia: Defence White Paper 2013*
- *The Military Strategy of the Republic of Lithuania 2012*
- *Australia in the Asian Century 2012*
- *Montenegro: Draft - National Security Strategy 2008*
- *Macedonia: White Paper on Defence 2012*
- *Philippines 2012: Transforming the Department of National Defence to Effectively Meet the Defence and Security Challenges of the 21st Century*
- *Spain: National Defence Directive 2012*
- *Norway: Future Acquisitions for the Norwegian Armed Forces 2012-2020*

- *Albania: Military Review 2012*
- *Latvia: The State Defence Concept 2012*
- *South Africa: Executive Authority's Overarching Annual Strategic Statement for 2012 (EA OASS)*
- *Japan: Defence of Japan 2012*
- *Lithuania: National Security Strategy 2012*
- *Georgia: National Security Concept of Georgia*
- *Hungary: Hungary's National Security Strategy*
- *Ireland: Strategy Statement 2011-2014*
- *Summary of National Defence Policy (Malaysia)*
- *Czech Republik: The Defence Strategy of the Czech Republic 2012*
- *Hungary's National Military Strategy 2012*
- *Ukraine: White Book 2011*
- *Canada: Report on Plans and Priorities 2012-13*
- *Philippines: National Security Policy*
- *Germany: Defence Policy Guidelines 2011*
- *Czech Republic: The White Paper on Defence 2011*
- *China: National Defence in 2010*
- *South Africa: Annual Performance Plan 2011*
- *South Africa: Strategic Plan 2011*
- *United States of America: The National Military Strategy 2011*
- *Brunei: Defence White Paper 2011*
- *Czech Republic: Security Strategy 2011*
- *South Africa: Overarching Strategic Statement for 2011*
- *Österreich: Weissbuch 2010*
- *Republic of China: National Defence Report 2011*
- *Ukraine: White Book 2010*
- *Lithuania: Defence Policy of Lithuania*
- *Japan: National Defence Program Guidelines for FY 2011 and Beyond*

- *New Zealand: Defence White Paper 2010*
- *Schweiz: Armeebericht 2010*
- *United Kingdom: A Strong Britain in an Age of Uncertainty*
- *Schweiz: Bericht des Bundesrates an die Bundesversammlung über die Sicherheitspolitik*
- *Estonia: National Security Concept 2010*
- *United States of America: The National Security Strategy*
- *Russia: The Military Doctrine*
- *Ukraine: White Book 2009*
- *Australia: Counter-Terrorism White Paper 2010*
- *South Africa: Strategic Plan 2010-2013*
- *South Korea: Defence White Paper 2010*
- *Chile: Libro de la Defensa Nacional 2010*
- *Serbia: Defence White Paper 2010*
- *Bulgaria: White Paper on Defence and the Armed Forces 2010*
- *Argentina: Libro Blanco de la Defensa*
- *NATO: 2010 Strategic Concept*
- *The Netherlands: Future Policy Survey 2010*
- *The Netherlands: Defence Doctrine 2010*
- *Vietnam: National Defence*
- *Ethiopia: Foreign Affairs and National Security Policy 2009*
- *Serbia: National Security Strategy 2009*
- *Denmark: Defence Agreement 2010 - 2014*
- *Russia: National Security Strategy to 2020*
- *Finland: Finnish Security and Defence Policy 2009*
- *China: National Defense in 2008*
- *Australia: Defence Capability Plan 2009*
- *Australia: Defence White Paper 2009*
- *Belize: The National Security Strategy 2009*
- *Österreich: Weissbuch 2008*
- *Poland: Defence Strategy 2009*
- *Estonia: Long-Term Defence Development Plan2009-2018*

- *Brazil: National Strategy of Defence*
- *South Korea: Defence White Paper 2008*
- *Montenegro: Draft - Defence Strategy 2008*
- *New Zealand: Defence Long-Term Development Plan 2008*
- *France: The French White Paper on Defence and National Security*
- *United States of America: The National Defence Strategy*
- *United Kingdom: The National Security Strategy*
- *Ukraine: White Book 2007*
- *Spain: National Defence Directive 2008*
- *Canada: Defence Strategy 2008*
- *Czech Republic: Military Strategy 2008*
- *Lithuania: Guidelines of the Minister of National Defence for 2009-2014*
- *Ireland: Strategy Statement 2008-2010*
- *Norway: Defence 2008*
- *Ireland: White Paper on Defence*
- *Ireland: The White Paper on Defence*
- *Turkey: Defence White Paper for 2007*
- *Azerbaijan: National Security Concept*

Indian Dilemma

Since the beginning of the Cold War, India suffered from three shortcomings. First, Nehru's relegating the economics of the market to a minor position in diplomacy; second, his inability to understand the inevitable onslaught of the potential power of an information age in the making; and third, the long period of Nehru's leadership as Prime Minister. Devoid of the realist approach to the world order, the Nehruvian vision resulted in the incorporation of world views that were based on the premise that there were only moral solutions to political problems. Translated into actual implementation, India incorporated central planning and state ownership in all strategic sectors of defence production and social welfare, including education under the garb of the mixed capitalistic economy. The private sector, thus, remained confined to consumer oriented consumable products production, which accounted for less than 30 percent of the total outlay for national development.

The private sector in this process lost the ability to have any stake related to national security, or a partnership in any form of decision-making on national security. There were no experts who could agree to disagree with Nehru publicly, either within the ruling party or its political adversaries, and survive. While Y B Chavan is a classic example of neutralisation by the then political architects, J R D Tata became the symbol of the insensitivity of the government towards the private sector. National interest in the post Nehru era was more or less ill defined by politicians and pursued by an unwieldy bureaucracy which perpetuated the "licence raj". The entire period of the Cold War, thus, saw the primacy of strategic policy-making based on privileged information on a need to know basis. India fell into the trap of relying on bureaucratic outlooks and perceptions and being ever suspicious of any free thinking by any non-governmental individual or organisation. So much so that even the Service Chiefs of the armed forces were seldom consulted. The sharing of information, mundane or otherwise, was a taboo and the private entrepreneurs were viewed as animals who were only interested in profit-making and hence, could not be patriotic, or trusted to safeguard national interests.

The only organisation, which was not government owned due to the Constitution and driven by the right to the freedom of speech was the national print media. Paradoxically, one comes across indirect evidence that the country was forced to be deprived of paper used for printing newspaper when adequate technology to manufacture the same was available in the country. This was to control the size of the newspapers to ensure limited writings representing differing viewpoints critically examining issues and perspectives on national as well as human security. Coupled with the lack of information related to strategic matters, the bureaucracy and the political leadership ensured that they remained in power by denying information to others which could be a basis of national debate on strategic perspectives. As is well known, the newsprint paper was imported and rationed under strict supervision. Even radio and television were under the state's supervision.

The Cultural Past

However, the Indian print media, with the capability to acquire information, thus, became a serious match for the bureaucrats having access to information. Under some of the famous editors/journalist like the late Girilal Jain, V G Varghese, Inder Malhotra and others, the national print media, through the editorial columns, became the conscience keepers for the Indian strategic rationale, and also the vehicle to articulate rationally the government's viewpoint. Interestingly, the era saw the rise of mavericks from amongst the civil servants on deputation to quasi non-governmental organisations patronised by the government. Some of these individuals created a "licence raj" to monopolise the entire gambit of strategic writings which were devoid of any research rigours. These writings were published in the national newspapers based more on insiders' knowledge of data or information and formed the core of reactive governmental view-points towards global strategic issues articulated by the strategic analysts around the world during the golden age of classical bipolarity. The entire exercise and practice had a major effect. It kept the authors limited and licensed in that the academia, the industries and the professionals from all non-governmental bodies were screened out from giving their opinions on national security. Needless to record that the mediocrity prevalent in the social science disciplines also contributed to this malady. The epitaph, therefore, went something like:

National security issues and deliberations are too serious a business to be indulged in by anyone else but those who have been authorized to do so by the government.

Defence analysis was preferred over security studies since the former based its premises on comparative military hardware/balances based on privileged data rather than indulging in security studies in which true power and the vitality of nation-state had to be calculated on the cultural and civilisational praxes incorporating the non-military/non-traditional dimensions of security (ecology, environment, pollution, energy, economic regimes, social and political and civil society institutions, along with the issues of human rights).

Proper incorporation of security studies in institutes of higher education, on one side, and allowing the corporate and private sector to have a stake in matters of security would have led to the evolution of strategic thinking to protect the core values and national interests of the nation. In the absence of such a paradigm, the bottom line of the entire development of the rationality of strategic thinking and projection of security perspectives was entrusted to a government organisation-centric empowered regime, which was constituted to ensure that strategically the country was administered to govern and not governed to administer. The virtual destruction of all democratic institutions in India during the Cold War period, including the political, was directly due to the political elites trying to establish committed organisations or individuals to safeguard the survival of the government in power. The worst incursion at the private individual level, which rattled the lowest common denominator in human security, was the imposition of forced sterilisation for furthering family planning.

Interestingly, no one, including those from the academic community, ever questioned as to why India had opted for a socialistic pattern of development despite the fact that democracy was practically an act of faith for the intelligent, and pursued a foreign policy which was operationalised and implemented by the MEA whose personnel, when posted in India, lived in Delhi, and when abroad, lived in the capital city of the country they were posted in. This highly 'competent' manpower that also spent its sabbatical years of leave of absence in the premier academic institutions of the Western world, remained far away from the real India. They had no competitors from within India and, hence, faced no challenge intellectually, professionally or organisationally. Realistically, they could be considered to be the real Non-Resident Indians (NRIs) all through the Cold War period. This paradigm had a telling effect on the rationale to imbibe prioritisation of human security over the traditional notions of security pursued in the 20th century.[53]

The Change

Much has changed today and there is hope and optimism in the air as the participation of agencies other than the state, on security and the discourse on strategy, has increased. Decentralisation of empowerment to 'think' has occurred. The media has taken centrestage to act as vigilante, and information is available to the people. Publication and writing on security matters has nearly exploded. Various commissions have taken centrestage and the government has tacitly decided to leave areas of involvement, which is none of its business to pursue ranging from running hotels, as it did in the past, to imparting professional education, with the Information Technology (IT) sector as a prime example. As the private universities are knocking on the door, even the Railways have started showing profits and announcing reward points, while Brookings, Carnagie, Oxford, London School of Economics (LSE), and similar institutions are seeking intellectual partnerships with private think-tanks and academic institutions where the government representatives are in attendance to learn and change their mindsets of the past. The success stories of the Mittals and Ambanis at the international and national domestic levels attract the best of minds for management and research and show the stake that the private sector will have in strategic areas of production and marketing. International relations and strategic partnerships in security issues will have strong economic ties as has been demonstrated in the recent developments in Indo-US nuclear cooperation in the civil and military domains. Both the scientists and the military have given valuable inputs for the government to act upon to forge a historic breakthrough which would have been well nigh impossible to even think about in the Cold War period. A definite role has been played by the media which has employed a number of former academics from institutes of higher education and are now working for the media with their studied writings and conducting well informed talk shows. As a matter of fact, the media has already started outsourcing strategic issue related debates on human security on a regular basis in which academics as well as political party spokespersons find their rightful place, demonstrating a new culture of protest as well as critical evaluation of policies on strategic and human security matters.

In Conclusion: The Way Ahead

There is a definite impact of neo-realism in India's approach to galvanise the national security policy-making strategy, supported by strategic thinking wherein the culture of strategic thinking has perceptively changed to become more realistic due to the participation of a variety of individuals, organisations and the private sector. The corporate sector giants have found a stake in national security affairs indirectly to safeguard their business interests in major areas like energy, the environment and intellectual property rights. Institutes of higher education have become sensitive to articulate issues on national security affairs through the conceptual lenses of various social science disciplines, using rigorous research methodologies documented with impeccable empirical evidence.

We are almost seeing the demise of the narrative analysis undertaken by the social science discipline and pursued in the last 50 years as an increasing variety of researchers belonging to the scientific community has started taking interest in articulating matters of "national security". The establishment of the first "National Centre of Strategic Studies" in an Indian university by the University Grants Commission (UGC), the ongoing endeavour over the years by the armed forces to establish the first National Defence University and similar efforts to create a strategic studies institute by the Indian Police Services and the three wings of the armed forces and the revamping of government supported think-tanks are indicative of a very healthy trend . It will not be long before these efforts will be brought to fruition as India needs studied inputs for developing a strategic culture to enable it to become a part of the knowledge society and global strategic equations. It appears that the long awaited shift from the habit of justifying our national security and foreign policy formulation will be replaced by policies framed by rational understanding of the international system, communicated to the international community by impeccable intellectual acumen. Lastly, we must recognise the Indian Diaspora, which has started influencing the emerging strategic cultural thinking in India from outside in a significant way. India is standing at the cross-roads of transformation where the institutes of higher education have to take the lead to bridge the gap between the concepts of human security and the strategic culture of the 20th century strategic imperatives. It is here that it becomes important to brainstorm and produce a roadmap for India, keeping in mind its cultural and civilisational praxis.

Strengthening the national security architecture will be possible if the triad of defence and strategic studies, defence studies and analyses, and national security policy-making become interdependent—organically, intellectually, professionally and systemically.[54] It also needs to be emphasised that "doctrine" as a term is loosely used. Doctrine is the crystallisation of concepts that in due course has the potential to yield policies. Also, there is an urgent need to compile a suitable lexicon of terms to be used in the domain of security and strategic studies. If India has to play its rightful role in global politics as a major power, then it is essential for it to develop world class human resources specialised in national security affairs. The schematic flowchart for this is given below.

The Indian Context: Constituting The Triad

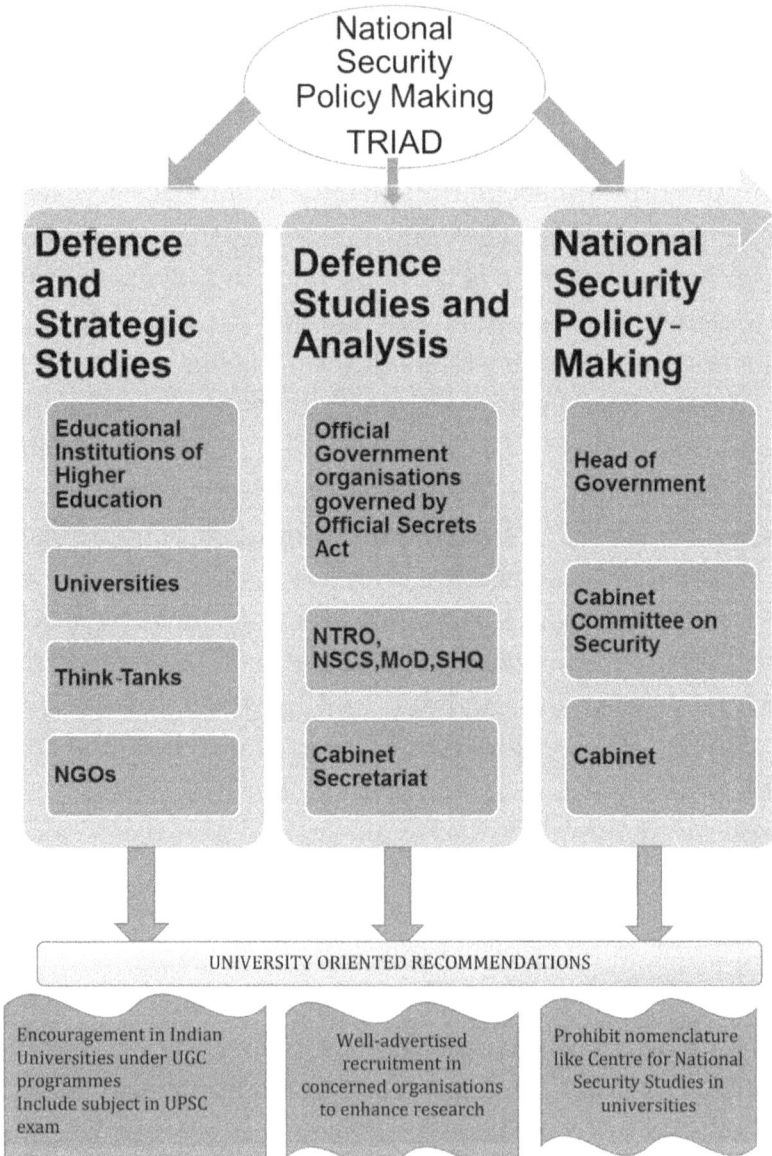

National Security Policy Making TRIAD

Defence and Strategic Studies

Educational Institutions of Higher Education

Universities

Think-Tanks

NGOs

Defence Studies and Analysis

Official Government organisations governed by Official Secrets Act

NTRO, NSCS,MoD,SHQ

Cabinet Secretariat

National Security Policy- Making

Head of Government

Cabinet Committee on Security

Cabinet

UNIVERSITY ORIENTED RECOMMENDATIONS

Encouragement in Indian Universities under UGC programmes Include subject in UPSC exam

Well-advertised recruitment in concerned organisations to enhance research

Prohibit nomenclature like Centre for National Security Studies in universities

NOTES

1. One specific reason for the feeble foreign policy of India is the structure of the Indian Foreign Service and the role it has played since 1947. See Manjari Chatterjee Miller, "India's Feeble Foreign Policy: A Would-Be Great Power Resists Its Own Rise", *Foreign Affairs*, May/June 2013. Similarly, see a very critical essay by Bharat Karnard, "India's Foreign Policy: The Foreign Hand — Has India Outsourced Foreign Policy to American Think-tanks"? *Open Magazine*, April 29, 2016. Also see Rahul Roy-Chaudhury, *Shifts and Changes in India's Foreign and Security Policy Under Modi* (2016), at http://www.iiss.org/en/iiss%20voices/blogsections/iiss-voices-2015-dda3/july-2632/shifts-and-changes-7c92, accessed on July 24, 2015. He identifies six shifts in the foreign and security policy of India during the present Modi government. See P M Kamath, "Nehru's Foreign Policy, Flawed and All", *Free Press Journal*, November 26, 2014. For referring to a complete compilation of India's Foreign Policy Documents, Government of India, see ten volumes compiled by Avtar Singh, *India's Foreign Relations Documents* (New Delhi: Public Diplomacy Division, Ministry of External Affairs, Geetika Publishers, 2011).

2. Gautam Sen, *Issue Brief*, No 81, Centre for Land Warfare Studies, July 2016

3. See Appendix - A.

4. Edward A. Kolodziej, "Renaissance in Security Studies? Caveat Lector", *International Quarterly*, Vol. 36, No.4, December 1992, pp. 421-438.

5. See Stephen M. Walt, "Renaissance of Security Studies", *International Studies Quarterly*, Vol. 35, No. 2, January 1991, pp. 211-239.

6. Francis Fukuyama, *The End Of History* (1989).
7. GLOBAL TRENDS vashu rak.pptx
8. The abstract of the Country Reports on Terrorism 2014 , United States Department of State, Publication Bureau of Counterterrorism, released June 2015, is important and is appended below:

    STRATEGIC ASSESSMENT

    Major trends in global terrorism in 2014 included the Islamic State in Iraq and the Levant's (ISIL's) unprecedented seizure of territory in Iraq and Syria, the continued flow of foreign terrorist fighters worldwide to join ISIL, and the rise of lone offender, violent extremists in the West. Despite the fragmentation of al-Qa'ida and its affiliates, weak or failed governance continued to provide an enabling the environment for the emergence of extremist radicalism and violence, notably in Yemen, Syria, Libya, Nigeria, and Iraq. Continuing a trend noted in last year's report, terrorist groups employed more aggressive tactics in their attacks. In ISIL's case, this included brutal repression of communities under its control and the use of ruthless methods of violence such as beheadings and crucifixions intended to terrify opponents. Boko Haram – operating in the Lake Chad Basin region of northern Nigeria, northern Cameroon, and southeast Niger – shared with ISIL a penchant for the use of brutal tactics, which included stonings, indiscriminate mass casualty attacks, and kidnapping children for enslavement. ISIL targeted religious minorities such as Christians and Yazidis in particular, but also Shia Muslims and Sunni tribesmen who defied its rule. The 2014 calendar year also witnessed a powerful regional and international mobilization to counter ISIL that halted the group's initial advances in Iraq. The adoption of UN Security Council Resolution 2178 in September constituted a significant step forward in international efforts to cooperate in preventing the flow of foreign terrorist fighters to and from conflict zones.

    The ongoing civil war in Syria was a significant factor in driving worldwide terrorism events in 2014. The rate of foreign terrorist fighter travel to Syria – totaling more than 16,000 foreign terrorist fighters from more than 90 countries as of late December – exceeded the rate of foreign terrorist fighters who traveled to Afghanistan and Pakistan, Iraq, Yemen, or Somalia at any point in the last 20 years. Many of the foreign terrorist fighters joined ISIL, which, through intimidation and exploitation of political grievances, a weak security environment in Iraq, and the conflict in Syria, secured sufficient support to conduct complex military operations in an effort to seize contiguous territory in western Iraq and eastern Syria for a self-declared Islamic caliphate. ISIL routinely and indiscriminately targeted defenseless civilians, including religious pilgrims, while engaging in violent repression of local inhabitants.

    ISIL showed a particular capability in the use of media and online products to address a wide spectrum of potential audiences: local Sunni Arab populations, potential recruits, and governments of coalition members and other populations around the world, including English-speaking audiences. ISIL has been adroit at using the most popular social and new media platforms (YouTube, Facebook, and Twitter) to disseminate its messages broadly, with near-instantaneous reposting and the generation of follow-on links and translations into additional languages following ISIL's initial publication of online propaganda. Content included brutal images, such as hostage beheadings and boasts of slave markets of Yazidi girls and women. In 2014, ISIL expanded its messaging tactics to include content that purported to show an idealized version of life under its rule and progress in building the institutions of an orderly state. ISIL's use of social and new media also facilitated its efforts to attract new recruits to the battlefields in Syria and Iraq, as ISIL facilitators answered in real time would-be members' questions about how to travel to join the group. Individuals drawn to the conflict in Syria and Iraq were diverse in their socioeconomic and geographic backgrounds, highlighting the need for comprehensive counter- messaging and early engagement with a variety of communities to dissuade vulnerable individuals from traveling to join the conflict.

In 2014, ISIL began to foster relationships with potential affiliates beyond Iraq and Syria. Ansar al- Shari'a in Darnah pledged allegiance to ISIL in October 2014, and Ansar Bayt al-Maqdis, operating primarily out of Egypt's Sinai Peninsula, officially declared allegiance to ISIL in November. Questions remained, however, about the meaning of such affiliates – whether representative of a command relationship, commonality of strategic goals, or merely opportunistic relationships.

The prominence of the threat once posed by core al-Qa'ida (AQ) diminished in 2014, largely as a result of continued leadership losses suffered by the AQ core in Pakistan and Afghanistan. AQ leadership also appeared to lose momentum as the self-styled leader of a global movement in the face of ISIL's rapid expansion and proclamation of a Caliphate.

Though AQ central leadership was weakened, the organization continued to serve as a focal point of "inspiration" for a worldwide network of affiliated groups, including al-Qa'ida in the Arabian Peninsula – a long-standing threat to Yemen, the region, and the United States; al-Qa'ida in the Islamic Maghreb; al-Nusrah Front; and al-Shabaab. Other violent Sunni Islamist extremist groups associated with AQ included the Islamic Jihad Union, Lashkar-i-Jhangvi, Harakat ul-Mujahadin, and Jemaah Islamiya. Tehrik-e Taliban Pakistan, the Afghan Taliban, and the Haqqani Network, which operated in Pakistan and Afghanistan, also have ties to AQ. Additionally, supporters and associates worldwide "inspired" by the group's ideology may have operated without direction from AQ central leadership, making it difficult to estimate their numbers.

Adherents of ISIL and AQ conducted terrorist attacks in the West in 2014 in so-called "lone offender attacks" including in Quebec and Ottawa, Canada (October 20 and October 22, respectively) and Sydney, Australia (December 15-16). In many cases, it was difficult to assess whether the attacks were directed or inspired by ISIL or by al-Qa'ida and its affiliates. These attacks may presage a new era in which centralized leadership of a terrorist organization matters less; group identity is more fluid; and violent extremist narratives focus on a wider range of alleged grievances and enemies with which lone actors may identify and seek to carry out self-directed attacks. Enhanced border security measures among Western states that have increased the difficulty for known or suspected terrorists to travel internationally likely encouraged groups like AQ and ISIL to inspire and rely on lone actors already resident in the West to carry out attacks and thereby realize their goal of terrorizing Western populations.

ISIL and AQ were far from the only serious threat that confronted the United States and its allies. Iran continued to sponsor terrorist groups around the world, principally through its Islamic Revolutionary Guard Corps-Qods Force (IRGC-QF). These groups included Lebanese Hizballah, several Iraqi Shia militant groups, Hamas, and Palestine Islamic Jihad. Iran, Hizballah, and other Shia militia continued to provide support to the Asad regime, dramatically bolstering its capabilities, prolonging the civil war in Syria, and worsening the human rights and refugee crisis there. Iran supplied quantities of arms to Syria and continued to send arms to Syria through Iraqi airspace in violation of UN Security Council Resolutions. Finally, Iran used Iraqi Shia militants and high profile appearances by Qods Force officials on the front lines of Iraq to claim credit for military successes against ISIL and to belittle coalition airstrikes and U.S. contributions to the Government of Iraq's ongoing fight against ISIL. ISIL and AQ affiliates, including al-Nusrah Front, continued to use kidnapping for ransom operations and other criminal activities to raise funds for operational purposes. Much of ISIL's funding, unlike that of AQ and AQ-type organizations, did not come from external donations but was internally gathered in Iraq and Syria. ISIL earned up to several million dollars per month through its various extortion networks and criminal activity in the territory where it operated, including through oil smuggling. Some progress was made in 2014 in constraining ISIL's ability to earn money from the sale of smuggled oil as a result of anti-ISIL coalition airstrikes that were conducted on ISIL-operated oil refineries.

President Obama has repeatedly stressed that the fight against terrorism is not one the United States can or should pursue alone. We have been working to shift our counterterrorism strategy to more effectively partner with countries where terrorist networks seek a foothold. Accordingly, we have built an effective Global Coalition to Counter ISIL; more than sixty partners are contributing to this multifaceted effort to stop ISIL's advances on the ground, combat the flow of foreign fighters, disrupt ISIL's financial resources, counteract ISIL's messaging, and undermine its appeal.

The shared foreign terrorist fighter threat has prompted even closer cooperation among U.S. federal agencies and our international partners, particularly in Europe. In September, President Obama chaired a UN Security Council (UNSC) session on the foreign terrorist fighter threat, and the UNSC subsequently adopted Resolution 2178. We have seen increased international focus on this problem and the development of more effective counterterrorism laws overseas, as well as enhanced border security efforts and a greater willingness to share threat information among partner nations.

Partners in North Africa and Asia also took steps in 2014 to strengthen their counterterrorism capabilities through new laws and the development of other means to identify, interdict, and prosecute foreign terrorist fighters and those who support them. Egypt, Jordan, Saudi Arabia, Qatar, Turkey, and the United Arab Emirates have all enacted legislation or regulations in 2014 to address the foreign terrorist fighter issue.

In West Africa, the countries of Cameroon, Chad, and Niger mobilized forces in 2014 to help Nigeria contain the growing threat posed by Boko Haram. With the authorization of the African Union (AU), these countries announced the launch of a new Multinational Joint Task Force to coordinate operations against Boko Haram. In Somalia, AU troops from Burundi, Djibouti, Ethiopia, Kenya, and Uganda continued to push al-Shabaab from towns, thus, supporting the people and government of Somalia's efforts to build security and stability

While countries worldwide worked to enact legislation and developed and implemented programs to address violent extremism, we remain concerned about counterproductive actions some governments have taken in the name of addressing terrorism – actions such as political repression and human rights violations, including extrajudicial killings, which could heighten political grievances and exacerbate the terrorist threat. These actions could become conditions that terrorists themselves exploit for recruitment – for example, banning political parties or suppressing freedom of speech by imprisoning bloggers and journalists. Multilateral and regional institutions can provide the appropriate framework to address these challenges.

9. See APPENDIX - B.

10. I have abridged this section from my reading on National Interest available at http://hass.unsw.adfa.edu.au/timor_companion/fracturing_the_bipartisan_consensus/national_interest.p hp

11. J Armstrong, *Nation Before Nationalism* (Chapel Hill: University of North Carolina Press, 1982).

12. A Smith, "The Origin of Nations", *Ethinic and Racial Studies*, Vol. 12., No. 3 1989.

13. B Anderson, *Imagined Communities*, (London: Verso, 1991), pp. 36-46.

14. J Frankel, *National Interest* (London: Pall Mall, 1970).

15. Ibid.

16. Ibid., p. 21.

17. E F Carr, *Nationalism and After* (London: MacMillan, 1945), pp. 2-6.

18. F. Meinecke, *Machiavellianism: The Doctrine of Raison d'État: Its Place in Modern History* (New Brunswick and London, 1998), p. 10.

19. Machiavelli (1961, 1999), pp. 50-57.

20. C. Beard, The Idea of National Interest: An Analytical Study in American *Foreign Policy* (New York: Macmillan, 1934), p. 155.

21. Ibid., p. 156.

22. Ibid.

23. Ibid., 157.
24. Rousseau (1960), p. 190.
25. Ibid.
26. Carr., n. 17, pp. 19-21.
27. J. Rosenau, "National Interest", in Sills D, *International Encyclopaedia of the Social Sciences* (New York: Crowell Collier and Macmillan, 1968).
28. Ibid.
29. Frankel, no. 14, pp. 31-32
30. Ibid., p. 33.
31. Ibid., p. 35.
32. R. Aron, *Peace and War* (London: Weidenfeld and Nicholson, 1966).
33. *Selected Works of Mao Zedong*, Vol. 5, (Peoples Press, 1977), p. 274.
34. *Selected Works of Deng Xiaoping*, Vol. 3 (People's Press, 1993), pp. 328-329.
35. Zhou Enlai, *Selection on Foreign Affairs* (Central Document Press, 1990), p. 2.
36. Like Panchsheel, the Gujral Doctrine also enshrined five principles: (i) with neighbouring states, India will take on the role of a donor to the maximum extent it can and will not ask anything in return; (ii) no South Asian country "will allow its territory to be used against the interests of another country in the region"; (iii) no one "will interfere with the internal affairs of another"; (iv) all South Asian countries "must respect each other's territorial integrity and sovereignty"; (v) all countries "will settle all their disputes through peaceful bilateral negotiations". See "Essential Tenets of Our Foreign Policy" *Mainstream*, January 15, 1997, quoted by Usha Thakkar and Mangesh Kulkarni, eds., *India In World Affairs: Towards The 21st Century* (Mumbai: Himalaya Publishing House, 1999), p. 77.
37. Sanjay Baru, "The Singh Doctrine", *The Indian Express*, November 06, 2013. Baru emphasises that there was indeed a Manmohan Singh Doctrine, with five components. First, India's relations with both major powers and its Asian neighbours are shaped by its "developmental priorities". Second, greater integration with the world economy is beneficial to India and to the realisation of the "creative potential" of the Indian people. Third, India needs "stable, long-term and mutually beneficial relations with all major powers". The fourth principle would be the building of stronger regional institutions to ensure greater regional cooperation and connectivity in "the Indian subcontinent". Fifth, underlying these "interests" are "values" represented by "India's experiment of pursuing economic development within the framework of a plural, secular and liberal democracy.
38. See Joseph Nye, *Understanding International Conflict: An Introduction to Theory and History* (New York: Harper & Collins, 1993).
39. An excellent exposition of the lack of long-term foreign policy planning is attributed to "New Delhi's dysfunctional foreign policy bureaucracy". National security policy-making has been totally dominated by former Foreign Service officers in their post retirement incarnation. This has been recorded in Miller, n. 1.
40. See Sen, n. 2.

41. Sardar Vallabhbhai Patel's letter to Jawaharlal Nehru on November 07, 1950, not only deplored Indian Ambassador KM Panikkar's action but also warned about dangers from China, In this letter, the Sardar postulated the following for immediate action:

    (a) A military and intelligence appreciation of the Chinese threat to India both on the frontier and to internal security.

    (b) An examination of the military position and such redisposition of our forces as might be necessary, particularly with the idea of guarding important routes or areas which are likely to be the subject of dispute.

    (c) An appraisement of the strength of our forces and, if necessary, reconsideration of our retrenchment plans for the Army in the light of the new threat.

    (d) A long-term consideration of our defence needs. My own feeling is that, unless we assure our supplies of arms, ammunition and armour, we would be making our defence perpetually weak and we would not be able to stand up to the double threat of difficulties both from the west and northwest and north and northeast.

    (e) The question of China's entry into the UN. In view of the rebuff which China has given us and the method which it has followed in dealing with Tibet, I am doubtful whether we can advocate its claim any longer. There would probably be a threat in the UN virtually to outlaw China, in view of its active participation in the Korean war. We must determine our attitude on this question also.

    (f) The political and administrative steps which we should take to strengthen our northern and northeastern frontier. This would include the whole of the border, ie. Nepal, Bhutan, Sikkim, Darjeeling and the tribal territory in Assam.

    (g) Measures of internal security in the border areas as well as the states flanking those areas such as Uttar Pradesh, Bihar, Bengal and Assam.

    (h) Improvement of our communication, road, rail, air and wireless, in these areas and with the frontier outposts.

    (i) The future of our mission at Lhasa and the trade posts at Gyangtse and Yatung and the forces which we have in operation in Tibet to guard the trade routes.

    (j) The policy in regard to the McMahon Line.

42. A P Rana, "The Nehruvian Tradition in World Affairs: Its Evolution and Relevance to Post Cold War International Relations" in Thakkar and Kulkarni eds., n. 36, p. 16.

43. Ibid., p.15.

44. S Menon, "Jawaharlal Nehru and World Order", 35th Jawaharlal Nehru Memorial Lecture, London, November 25, 2014, p., 3. He further observes in the same lecture "By the late fifties, JN's ideas on the world order and his foreign policy practice were eminently compatible with Wilsonian liberal internationalism. This was not out of woolly headed idealism but out of a

conviction that a fairer international order would help to mitigate the asymmetry of power that had formed the post-War order, and, thus, serve India's needs"

45. Thakkar and Kulkarni, n. 36, p. 2.

46. Menon, n. 44, p. 8.

47. See AP Rana, "Understanding International Conflicts in the Third World: A Conceptual Enquiry", *International Studies,* April-June 1996.

48. Miller, n. 1, pp. 1-4.

49. Ibid.

50. Rajesh M Basrur, "Indian Foreign Policy and International Relations Theory: A Post-Neorealist View", in Thakkar and Kulkarni, eds., n. 36, p. 34.

51. Ibid., p.35, as quoted from Kenneth N Waltz, *Theory of International Politics,* (Reading, MA: Addison-Wesley, 1979).

52. The notion of non-alignment or whatever was left, saw its demise when a group of public intellectuals tried to resurrect it in 2012. See Sunil Khilani, Rajiv Kumar et. al., eds., *NONALIGNMENT 2.0: A Foreign and Strategic Policy For India in the Twenty First Century,* printed and published in India 2012. The publication does not indicate the name or the place of the printers nor was it placed on sale. However, it records, "The views, findings and recommendations of this document are the product of collective deliberation by an independent group of analysts and policy-makers: Sunil Khilnani, Rajiv Kumar, Pratap Bhanu Mehta, Lt. Gen. (Retd.) Prakash Menon, Nandan Nilekani, Srinath Raghavan, Shyam Saran, Siddharth Varadarajan. The group's activities were administratively supported by the National Defence College and Centre for Policy Research, New Delhi. This document does not represent the views of either of these institutions, their faculty or their administration. Nor does it represent the views of any of the institutions with which the authors of the document are affiliated. All statements of fact and expressions of opinion contained in this document are the sole responsibility of the authors." The publication was timed and released just before the Indian Prime Minister was to attend the Seoul Nuclear Summit. The release of this document in Ashoka Hotel, New Delhi, was attended by Shri Brijesh Mishra and Shri M K Narain, both former National Security Advisers, and Shri Shiv Shankar Menon, the then National Security Adviser. All of them spoke on the occasion. Following the release, there was severe criticism from the academic and strategic community of India, leading to its contents and context being totally invalidated. One Indian university, in 2013, carried out a full scale seminar attended by one of the principle authors giving a keynote address. Even there, the publication did not find any takers amongst the students and academic faculty. See comments by Gautam Sen, Presidential Address, National Seminar on Non-alignment 2.0 in the Department of Civics & Politics, University of Mumbai, January 21-22, 2013. It observed that despite the report being crafted by a distinguished group of scholars and former government officials, the shortcomings in the report needs to be tabulated: (1) The report is a reiteration of the old Nehruvian/ Liberal perspective on foreign and strategic policy making. (2) The report, thus,

aims to justify the continuity of present Indian policies and, hence, does not take into account the centrality of the balance of power politics, which will continue to be a key factor in inter-state relations at regional and global levels in the 21st century. (3) The report lays stress on India to exhibit the role of an exemplar by recording that " the fundamental source of Indian power in the world is going to be the power of its example". In other words, it is the "moral" rather than the material means which will enable India to achieve global status. Any student of real politik would know that morality and the power of example is of hardly any consequence in the arena of international politics of today. It is evident that the 'moral imperative' has been too much emphasised in the report in the quest for power. (4) The report fails to record that India's position in global ranking is not because of its moralistic stands on international issues but because of its growth in every known area of indices which contributes in the calculation of the potential to power. (5) The report is uncomfortable with the power status of the United States as one which is more powerful than the others. The report clearly indicates that the Indian government at all times has not been able to come to terms with the global balance of power politics. It would appear by studying Non-Alignment 2.0 that the Indian policy-making infrastructure tried to retain the ability to reject the policy thrust contained in "Non-Alignment 2.0" should there be a political backlash from the opposition political parties. True, as an earlier commentator has recorded that the US sees " China and India as entirely different cups of tea" and considers that "USA does not understand the vast humanity of China and India having their own national interest." I can definitely give credit to the Chinese to have defined their national interest. In the case of India, it is far from either being quantified, debated or a consensus arrived at. This is evident from the Indian document citing " India's national interest being too complex". It surely indicates a lack of consensus on defining national interest in India. This is specifically due to the reason that the process of bridging the gap between the realm of ideas and the domain of public policy-making has never been achieved nor attempted in India. The potential soft power incubators i.e. the academic community, the writers and thinkers outside the government agencies have hardly been consulted, made to act as stakeholders or allowed to be part of deliberations for policy-making.

53. A useful reading list is placed as APPENDIX - C.
54. Sen, n. 2.

APPENDIX - A

IR Paradigms: Approaches and Theories

Balance of Power Theory

As a theory, balance of power predicts that rapid changes in international power and status—especially attempts by one state to conquer a region—will provoke counter-balancing actions. For this reason, the balancing process helps to maintain the stability of relations between states. A balance of power system functions most effectively when alliances are fluid, when they are easily formed or broken on the basis of expediency, regardless of values, religion, history, or form of government. Occasionally a single state plays a balancer role, shifting its support to oppose whatever state or alliance is strongest. A weakness of the balance of power concept is the difficulty of measuring power. (Extract from "Balance of Power," Microsoft® Encarta® Online Encyclopedia 2000 http://encarta.msn.com © 1997-2000 Microsoft Corporation. All rights reserved.)

Behaviouralism

This is an approach to the study of politics or other social phenomena that focusses on the actions and interactions among units by using scientific methods of observation to include quantification of variables whenever possible. A practitioner of behaviouralism is often referred to as a behaviouralist. Behaviourism refers to the ideas held by those behavioral scientists who consider only observed behavior as relevant to the scientific enterprise and who reject what they consider to be metaphysical notions of "mind" or "consciousness" [P. Viotti, and M. Kauppi, eds., *International Relations Theory* (New York: Macmillan Publishing Company, 1987)].

Chaos Theory

In mathematics and physics, the chaos theory describes the behaviour of certain non-linear dynamical systems that may exhibit dynamics that are highly sensitive to initial conditions (popularly referred to as the butterfly effect). As a result of this sensitivity, which manifests itself as an exponential growth of perturbations in the initial conditions, the behaviour of chaotic systems appears to be random. This happens even though these systems are deterministic, meaning that their future dynamics are fully defined by their initial conditions, with no random elements involved. This behaviour is known as deterministic chaos, or simply chaos. Since the international system can be considered a non-linear dynamic system, it is reasonable to take this theory into account for the study of the international order. (Mostly from Wikipedia.)

Classical Realism

Also called human realism and associated with Morgenthau's exposition of realism in which the power pursuit propensity of states is derived from the basic nature of human beings as power maximisers. This perspective holds that ideological, as well as material, factors may constitute 'power' (e.g. power over public opinion) and, hence, has some social underpinning.

Collective Defence

Though the term existed before 1949, a common understanding of collective defence with regards to NATO can be found in Article V of the North Atlantic Treaty: "The Parties agree that an armed attack against one or more of them... shall be considered an attack against them all; and, consequently, they agree that if such an armed attack occurs, each of them, in exercise of the right of individual or collective self-defence, recognised by Article 51 of the Charter of the United Nations, will assist the Party or Parties so attacked by taking forthwith, individually and in concert with the other Parties, such action as it deems necessary, including the use of armed force, to restore and maintain the security of the North Atlantic area" (NATO Handbook: 232). In the context of NATO, then, collective defence is based on countering traditional challenges as understood by the realist/neo-realist paradigm, specifically to territory, and finds its focus on an identifiable external threat or adversary.

Collective Security
Employed during the construction of the League of Nations, the concept of collective security goes beyond the pure idea of defence to include, according to Inis Claude, "arrangements for facilitating peaceful settlement of disputes," assuming that the mechanisms of preventing war and defending states under armed attack will "supplement and reinforce each other" (1984:245). Writing during the Cold War, Claude identifies the concept as the post-World War I name given by the international community to the "system for maintenance of international peace... intended as a replacement for the system commonly known as the balance-of-power" (1984:247). Most applicable to widely inclusive international organisations such as the League and the United Nations, ideally, the arrangement would transcend the reliance on deterrence of competing alliances through a network or scheme of "national commitments and international mechanisms." As in collective defence, collective security is based on the risk of retribution, but it can also involve economic and diplomatic responses, in addition to military retribution. From this, it is theorised that perfected collective security would discourage potential aggressors from angering a collectivity of states. Like balance-of-power, collective security works on the assumption that any potential aggressor would be deterred by the prospect of joint retaliation, but it goes beyond the military realm to include a wider array of security problems. It assumes that states will relinquish sovereignty and freedom of action or inaction to increasing interdependence and the premise of the indivisibility of peace. The security that can be derived from this is part of the foundation of the neoliberal institutionalist argument.

Communitarianism

Complex Adaptive Systems Theory

Complex Interdependence Theory
The term 'complex interdependence' was developed by Robert Keohane and Joseph Nye and refers to the various, complex transnational connections (interdependencies) between states and societies. Interdependence theorists noted that such relations, particularly economic ones, were increasing; while the use of military force and power balancing were decreasing (but remained important). Reflecting

on these developments, they argued that the decline of military force as a policy tool and the increase in economic and other forms of interdependence should increase the probability of cooperation among states. The complex interdependence framework can be seen as an attempt to synthesise elements of realist and liberal thought. Finally, anticipating problems of cheating and relative gains raised by realists, interdependence theorists introduced the concept of 'regimes' to mitigate anarchy and facilitate cooperation. Here, we can see an obvious connection to neo-liberal institutionalism. See R. Keohane, and J. Nye, *Power and Interdependence: World Politics in Transition* (Boston: Little-Brown, 1977), 2nd edition,1989.

Complexity Theory

Constitutional Order Theory

Philip Bobbitt's central thesis (in his book *The Shield of Achilles*, 2002) is that the interplay between strategic and constitutional innovation changes the constitutional order of the state. In putting his thesis, Bobbitt also contends that epochal wars have brought a particular constitutional order to primacy; a constitutional order achieves dominance by best exploiting the strategic and constitutional innovations of its era; the peace treaties that end epochal wars ratify a particular constitutional order for the society of states; and each constitutional order asserts a unique basis for legitimacy. In terms of the current international system, Bobbitt argues that it is transitioning from an order of nation-states to market- states. The value of Bobbitt's thesis is that it better explains relations between states, as well as changes within states and in the international system, than the (previously) dominant theory of neo-realism, which assumes that all states are the same and seek only to survive in an anarchical and competitive system through on-going power balancing.

Constitutive Theory

Constitutive theory is directly concerned with the importance of human reflection on the nature and character of world politics and the approach to its study. Reflections on the process of theorising, including epistemological and ontological issues and questions, are typical. Constitutive theory is distinguished from explanatory or empirical theory (see below) and may be described as the *philosophy* of world politics or international relations.

Constructivism

Constructivist theory rejects the basic assumption of neo-realist theory that the state of anarchy (lack of a higher authority or government) is a structural condition inherent in the system of states. Rather, it argues, in Alexander Wendt's words, "Anarchy is what states make of it". That is, anarchy is a condition of the system of states because states in some sense 'choose' to make it so. Anarchy is the result of a process that constructs the rules or norms that govern the interaction of states. The condition of the system of states today as self-helpers in the midst of anarchy is a result of the process by which states and the system of states were constructed. It is not an inherent fact of state-to-state relations. Thus, constructivist theory holds that it is possible to change the anarchic nature of the system of states. (See Alexander Wendt, "Anarchy is What States Make of It," *International Organization,* 46, 2, Spring 1992.

Corporatism

Critical Social Theory

This is not really a theory, but an approach or methodology which seeks to take a critical stance towards itself by, firstly, recognising its own presuppositions and role in the world; and, secondly, towards the social reality that it investigates by providing grounds for the justification and criticism of the institutions, practices and mentalities that make up that reality. Critical social theory, therefore, attempts to bridge the divides in social thought between explanation and justification, philosophical and substantive concerns, pure and applied theory, and contemporary and earlier thinking.

Cultural Internationalism

Decision- Making Analysis

Defensive Realism

Defensive realism is an umbrella term for several theories of international politics and foreign policy that build upon Robert Jervis' writings on the security dilemma and to a lesser extent upon Kenneth Waltz's balance-of-power theory (neo-realism). Defensive realism holds that the international system provides incentives for expansion only under certain conditions. Anarchy (the absence of a universal sovereignor worldwide government) creates situations whereby the tools that one state uses to increase its security, decrease the security of other states. This security dilemma causes states to worry about one another's future intentions and relative power. Pairs of states may pursue purely security seeking strategies, but inadvertently generate spirals of mutual hostility or conflict. States often, although not always, pursue expansionist policies because their leaders mistakenly believe that aggression is the only way to make their state secure. Defensive realism predicts great variation in internationally driven expansion and suggests that states ought to generally pursue moderate strategies as the best route to security. Under most circumstances, the stronger states in the international system should pursue military, diplomatic, and foreign economic policies that communicate restraint. Examples of defensive realism include: offence-defence theory (Jervis, Stephen Van Evera, Sean Lynn-Jones, and Charles Glaser), balance-of-power theory (Barry Posen, Michael Mastanduno), balance-of-threat theory (Stephen Walt), domestic mobilisation theories (Jack Snyder, Thomas Christensen, and Aron Friedberg), and security dilemma theory (Thomas Christensen, Robert Ross, and William Rose). Sources: Jeffrey W. Taliaferro, "Security-Seeking Under Anarchy: Defensive Realism Reconsidered," *International Security*, 25, 3, Winter 2000/2001: 152-86; and John J. Mearsheimer, *Tragedy of Great Power Politics* (New York: W.W. Norton, 2002).

Democratic Peace

All democratic peace theories seek to explain the disputed empirical fact that two constitutional democracies have never gone to war with each other in recent history (1816 onwards). As such, they rest on a similar hypothesis: that relations between pairings of democratic states are inherently more peaceful than relations between other regime-type pairings (i.e. democratic versus non-democratic or non-democratic versus non-democratic). To prove the reality of the democratic peace, theorists such as Michael Doyle have sought to show a causal relationship between the independent variable—"democratic political structures at the unit level" and the dependent variable—"the asserted absence of war between democratic states". Critics such as Ido Oren, dispute the claims of democratic peace theorists by insisting that there is a liberal bias in the interpretation of 'democracy' which weakens the evidence.

APPENDIX - A | 85

Dependency Theory

Dependency theorists assert that so-called 'third world' countries were not always 'poor', but became impoverished through colonial domination and forced incorporation into the world economy by expansionist 'first world' powers. Thus, 'third world' economies became geared more toward the needs of their 'first world' colonial masters than the domestic needs of their own societies. Proponents of dependency theory contend that relationships of dependency have continued long after formal colonisation ended. Thus, the primary obstacles to autonomous development are seen as external rather than internal, and so 'third world' countries face a global economy dominated by rich industrial countries. Because 'first world' countries never had to contend with colonialism or a world full of richer, more powerful competitors, dependency theorists argue that it is unfair to compare contemporary 'third world' societies with those of the 'first world' in the early stages of development.

Deterrence Theory

Deterrence is commonly thought about in terms of convincing opponents that a particular action would elicit a response resulting in unacceptable damage that would outweigh any likely benefit. Rather than a simple cost/benefit calculation, however, deterrence is more usefully thought of in terms of a dynamic process, with provisions for continuous feedback. The process initially involves determining who shall attempt to deter whom from doing what, and by what means. Several important assumptions underlie most thinking about deterrence. Practitioners tend to assume, for example, that states are unitary actors, and logical according to Western concepts of rationality. Deterrence also assumes that we can adequately understand the calculations of an opponent. One of the most important assumptions during the Cold War was that nuclear weapons were the most effective deterrent to war between the states of the East and the West. This assumption, carried into the post-Cold War era, however, may promote nuclear proliferation. Indeed, some authors suggest that the spread of nuclear weapons would deter more states from going to war against one another. The weapons would, it is argued, provide weaker states with more security against attacks by stronger neighbours. Of course, this view is also predicated on the assumption that every state actor's rationality will work against the use of such weapons, and that nuclear arms races will, therefore, not end in nuclear warfare. [Edited extract from *Post-Cold War Conflict Deterrence* (Naval Studies Board, National Research Council, National Acadamy of Sciences, 1997.)]

Dialectical Functionalism

Domino Theory

Dynamic Interaction Theory

Emancipatory International Relations
Emancipatory International Relations (IR) are characterised by a number of schools of thought most broadly falling under the umbrella of Wesern or Hegelian Marxism, such as neo-Gramscian theory and approaches to IR based on the Frankfurt School philosophy. These approaches to emancipatory IR can be shown to be reformist rather than revolutionary, in the sense that visions of an alternative world order fail to transcend the state. Thus, some would suggest that approaches to IR that are derived from an anarchist political philosophy, for example, are more appropriate for an emancipatory conception of IR which is revolutionary rather than reformist.

Empirical Theory
An empirical theory in the social or natural sciences relates to facts and provides an explanation or prediction for observed phenomena. Hypotheses associated with empirical theories are subject to test against real-world data or facts. The theorist need not have any purpose in developing such empirical theories other than satisfying his or her intellectual curiosity, although many will seek to make their work "policy relevant" [P. Viotti and M. Kauppi, eds., *International Relations Theory* (New York: Macmillan Publishing Company, 1987)].

Ethnic Conflict Theory
Ethnic conflicts are old. Violence has been used for state recognition, autonomy or to join a neighbouring state. Such conflicts received serious attention by scholars in the aftermath of the Cold War and with the demise of the former Yugoslavia and USSR into several independent states. Ethnic conflict studies can be a source for understanding international

relations bearing in mind that no single book, concept or theory can expect to capture such a complex phenomenon in its entirety. Political scientists use concepts and theories of sociologists such as Evans (1993), Giddens (1993), Smith (1986), Rex (1986), Hurd (1986) and Laitin (1986) to explain endemic ethnic conflicts caused by alienation and deprivation of ethnic minority groups bonded by history, descent, language, religion and culture, living in a defined territory. This group perceives itself as 'me-you,' 'we-they,' 'insiders-outsiders,' and 'minority-majority.' T h e r e a r e three contending ethnic conflict theories: (a) primordialists stress the importance of instinctive behaviour of belonging; (b) instrumentalist or circumstantialists cite compelling socio-economic-political factors; and (c) constructivists point to the social nature of ethnic groups. For ethnic conflict management models of political 'accommodation' or 'arrangements', see Walker, C. 1994, *Ethnocentrisvm: The Quest for Understanding* (Chapters 6 & 8) (Princeton University Press); J. McGarry and O'Leary, B. eds., *The Politics of Ethnic Conflict Resolution: Case Studies of Protracted Ethnic Conflicts* (Chapter 1), (Routledge, 1993); and A. Lijphart, *Democracy in Plural Societies* (Chapters 1 & 2) (Yale University Press, 1997). For further perspectives, see M. Toft, *The Geography of Ethnic Violence: Identity, Interests, and the Indivisibilty of Territory* (Princeton University Press, 2003); B. Anderson, *Imagined Communities: Reflections on the Origin and Spread of Nationalism* (Verso, 1991); and P. Huntington, *The Clash of Civilizations and the Remaking of World Order* (Simon & Schuster,1996).

Evolutionary World Politics

This is a sub-field of the study of international relations that poses the question: what explains structural change in world politics, in the past millennium, in particular? It rests on two core premises: that political change at the global level is the product of evolutionary processes, and that such processes might be best understood through the application of evolutionary concepts such as selection or learning, without yet embracing biological determinism. Focussing on longer-term, institutional change, it contrasts with, and complements, rational choice approaches that illuminate shorter-term, ends-means decision-making. Components of it might be recognised in both the realist, and the liberal schools of international relations. Structural change may be studied at three levels: at the actor level, by looking at long cycles of global politics; at the level of global political formation, by inquiring into the world empire, the nation-state system with global leadership, and global organisation, as alternative forms of coping with global problems; and at the level of human species evolution, by asking about the emergence of basic world institutions. Global political change co-evolves with cognate processes in the world economy, and is nested in the longer-term developments in democratisation, and changes in world opinion. For recent research, reports and bibliography, see The Evolutionary World Politics Home Page.

Feminism

This is a branch of critical social theory (see above) that seeks to explore how we think, or do not think, or avoid thinking about gender in International Relations (IR). Feminists argue that traditional IR thinking has avoided thinking of *men* and *women* in the capacity of embodied and socially constituted subject categories by subsuming them in other categories (e.g. statesmen, soldiers, refugees), too readily accepting that women are located inside the typically separate sphere of domestic life, and retreating to abstractions (i.e. the state) that mask a masculine identity. Gender-minded analysts, therefore, seek to move from suspicion of officially ungendered IR texts to their subversion and to replacement theories. Some recent gender-attentive research streams include: critique and reappropriation of stories told about the proper scope of the field of IR; revisions of war and peace narratives; reevaluations of women and development in the international system and its parts; feminist interpretations of human rights; and feminist understandings of international political economy and globalisation. (These notes are an adaptation of a piece by Christine Sylvester: "Feminist Theory and Gender Studies in International Relations").

Fourth World Theory

Comprising a theoretical framework, the Fourth World Theory is based on the distinction between nations and states, examining how colonial empires and modern states invaded and now encapsulate most of the world's enduring peoples. The term *Fourth World* refers to nations forcefully incorporated into states which maintain a distinct political culture but are internationally unrecognised (R. Griggs. "The Meaning of 'Nation' and 'State' in the Fourth World", Centre for World Indigenous Studies, 1992). Fourth World analyses, writings and maps aim to rectify the distorting and obscuring of indigenous nations' identities, geographies and histories, and expose the usually hidden 'other side' of invasions and occupations that generate most of the world's wars, refugees, genocide, human rights violations and environmental destruction. The distinction between political terms such as nation, state, nation-state, people and ethnic group, which are commonly used interchangeably in both popular and academic literature despite the fact that each has a unique connotation, provides a geopolitical perspective from which one can paint a 'ground-up' portrait of the significance and centrality of people in most world issues, problems and solutions. The Fourth World Theory was fashioned by a diverse assortment of people, including activists, human rights lawyers, academics and leaders of indigenous nations. Similar to World Systems Analysis (see below) scholars and proponents of the Fourth World Theory seek to change the world, not just describe or explain it.

Frustration-Aggression Theory
A theory that argues that collective behaviour is an aggressive response to feelings of frustration.

Functionalism
Functionalism is a focus on purposes or tasks, particularly those performed by organisations. Some theorists have explained the growth of organisations, particularly international organisations, as a response to an increase in the number of purposes or tasks demanding attention. *Neo-functionalism* as a theory of regional integration emphasises the political calculation and pay-off to elites who agree to collaborate in the performance of certain tasks [P. Viotti and M. Kauppi, eds., *International Relations Theory* (New York: Macmillan Publishing Company, 1987)].

Game Theory
This is a decision-making approach based on the assumption of actor rationality in a situation of competition. Each actor tries to maximise gains or minimise losses under conditions of uncertainty and incomplete information, which requires each actor to rank order preferences, estimate probabilities, and try to discern what the other actor is going to do. In a two-person *zero-sum* game, what one actor wins, the other loses; if A wins 5, B loses 5, and the sum is zero. In a two-person *non-zero* or *variable sum* game, gains and losses are not necessarily equal;

it is possible that both sides may gain. This is sometimes referred to as a *positive-sum* game. In some games, both parties can lose, and by different amounts or to a different degree. So-called *n-person* games include more than two actors or sides. Game theory has contributed to the development of models of deterrence and arms race spirals, but it is also the basis for work concerning the question of how collaboration among competitive states in an anarchic world can be achieved: The central problem is that the rational decision for an individual actor such as a state may be to 'defect' and go it alone as opposed to taking a chance on collaboration with another state actor. Dealing with this problem is a central concern of much of the literature on international regimes, regional integration, and conflict resolution [P. Viotti and M. Kauppi, eds., *International Relations Theory* (New York: Macmillan Publishing Company, 1987)].

Globalisation

Globalisation, as a theory, argues that states and societies are increasingly being 'disciplined' to behave as if they are private markets operating in a global territory. 'Disciplinary' forces affecting states and societies are attributed to the global capital market, Transnational Corporations (TNCs), and structural adjustment policies of the International Monetary Fund (IMF) and World Bank, which are all driven by the neo-liberal economic ideology. Some scholars, such as Stephen Gill, see these agents as representing an emerging system of global economic governance ('disciplinary neo-liberalism') based on a quasi-constitutional framework for the reconstitution of the legal rights, prerogatives, and freedom of movement for capital on a world scale ('new constitutionalism'). See S. Gill, "New Constitutionalism, Democratisation and Global Political Economy", *Pacifica Review,* January 10, 1998.

Globalism

This is an image of politics different from *realism* and *pluralism*. Globalism focusses on the importance of the economy, especially capitalist relations of dominance or exploitation, for an understanding of world politics. The globalist image is influenced by Marxist analyses of exploitative relations, although not all globalists are Marxists. The dependency theory, whether understood in Marxist or non-Marxist terms, is categorised here as part of the globalist image. Also included is the view that international relations are best understood if one sees them as occurring within a world-capitalist system. [P. Viotti and M. Kauppi, eds., *International Relations Theory* (New York: Macmillan Publishing Company, 1987)].

Golden Arches Theory of Conflict Prevention

Thomas Friedman's theory is that no two countries that had McDonald's had fought a war against each other ever since each got its McDonald's. More specifically, Friedman articulates it thus: "When a country reached the level of economic development where it had a middle class big enough to support a McDonald's network, it became a McDonald's country. And people in McDonald's countries didn't like to fight wars anymore, they preferred to wait in line for burgers". [See Chapter 12 in Thomas L. Friedman, *The Lexus and The Olive Tree* (London: Harper Collins Publishers, 2000)].

Gramscianism

Hegemonic Stability Theory

The central idea of this theory is that the stability of the international system requires a single dominant state to articulate and enforce the rules of interaction among the most important members of the system. For a state to be a hegemon, it must have three attributes: the capability to enforce the rules of the system, the will to do so, and a commitment to a system which is perceived as mutually beneficial to the major states. A hegemon's capability rests upon the likes of a large, growing economy, dominance in a leading technological or economic sector, and political power backed up by projective military power. An unstable system will result if economic, technological, and other changes erode the international hierarchy and undermine the position of the dominant state. Pretenders to hegemonic control will emerge if the benefits of the system are viewed as unacceptably unfair. (Extract from lecture notes on the theory of hegemonic stability by Vincent Ferraro, Ruth C. Lawson Professor of International Politics at Mount Holyoke College, Massachusetts.)

Historical Internationalism

Historical Materialism

Historical Sociology

Idealism

Idealism is so widely defined that only certain basic tenets can be described. Idealists believe strongly in the affective power of ideas, in that it is possible to base a political system primarily on morality, and that the baser and more selfish impulses of humans can be muted in order to build national and international norms of behaviour that foment peace, prosperity, cooperation, and justice. Idealism then is not only heavily reformist, but the tradition has often attracted those who feel that idealistic principles are the "next step" in the evolution of the human character. One of the first and foremost pieces of the "old world" and "old thinking" to be tossed on the trash heap of history by idealism is that destructive human institution of war. War, in the idealistic view, is now no longer considered by either elites or the populace of the great powers as being a plausible way of achieving goals, as the costs of war, even for the victor, exceed the benefits. As John Mueller says in his book *Quiet Cataclysm*, war is passing into that consciousness stage where slavery and duelling reside—it can fade away without any adverse effect, and with no need for replacement.

Imperialism

Hans J. Morgenthau defines imperialism as a national foreign policy aimed at acquiring more power than the state actually has, through a reversal of existing power relations, in other words, a favourable change in power status. Imperialism as a national foreign policy is in contrast to a 'status quo' foreign policy and a foreign policy of 'prestige.' The policy of imperialism assumes the classical realist theory perspective of analysis at the unit level in international relations. Furthermore, imperialism is based on a 'balance-of-power' construct in international relations. The three types of imperialism as outlined by Morgenthau are: Marxist theory of imperialism which rests on the foundation that all political phenomena are the reflection of economic forces; the liberal theory of imperialism which results because of maladjustments in the global capitalist system (e.g., surplus of goods and capital which seek outlets in foreign markets); and, finally, the 'devil' theory of imperialism which posits that manufacturers and bankers plan wars in order to enrich themselves. From Hans J. Morgenthau, *Politics Among Nations: The Struggle for Power and Peace* (Boston: McGraw-Hill, 1948) (Chapter 5, The Struggle for Power: Imperialism).

Incrementalism

Integration Theory

Inter-governmentalism

In its most basic form, inter-governmentalism explains inter-state cooperation and especially regional integration (e.g. the EU) as a function of the alignment of state interests and preferences coupled with power. That is, contrary to the expectations of functionalism and neo-functionalism, integration and cooperation are actually caused by rational self-interested states bargaining with one another. Moreover, as would be expected, states with more 'power' are likely to have more of their interests fulfilled. For example, with regard to the EU, it is not surprising, according to proponents of this theory, that many of the agreed-upon institutional arrangements are in line with the preferences of France and Germany, the so-called 'Franco-German core.' Andrew Moravcsik is probably the most well-known proponent of inter-governmentalism right now. (See, for example, Andrew Moravcsik, "Preferences and Power in the European Community: A Liberal Intergovernmentalist Approach," *Journal of Common Market Studies*, December 1993.)

Internationalism

Internationalism is a political movement that advocates greater economic and political cooperation among participating actors for the benefit of all. It is by nature opposed to ultranationalism, jingoism and national chauvinism and presupposes the recognition of other nations as equal, in spite of all their differences. Indeed, it is most commonly expressed as an appreciation for the diverse cultures in the world and as a desire for world peace. It also encompasses an obligation to assist the world through leadership and cooperation, advocating robust global governance and the presence of international organisations such as the United Nations.

International Order Theory

International Political Economy

A method of analysis concerning the social, political and economic arrangements affecting the global systems of production, exchange and distribution, and the mix of values reflected therein [S. Strange, *States and Markets* (London: Pinter Publishers, 1988, p. 18)]. As an analytical method, political economy is based on the assumption that what occurs in the economy reflects, and affects, social power relations.

International Regime Theory

This comprises a perspective that focusses on cooperation among actors in a given area of international relations. An international regime is viewed as a set of implicit and explicit principles, norms, rules, and procedures around which actors' expectations converge in a particular issue-area. An issue-area comprises interactions in such diverse areas as nuclear non-proliferation, telecommunications, human rights, or environmental problems. A basic idea behind international regimes is that they provide for transparent state behaviour and a degree of stability under conditions of anarchy in the international system. International regime analysis has been offering a meeting ground for the debate between the various schools of thought in international relations theory. See S.Krasner, *International Regimes* (Ithaca: Cornell University Press, 1983).

Just War Theory

Normative theory referring to conditions under which (1) states rightfully go to war *(jus ad bellum)* with a just cause, as in self-defence in response to aggression, when the decision to go to war is made by the legitimate authority in the state as a last resort after exhausting peaceful remedies, *and* with some reasonable hope of achieving legitimate objectives; (2) states exercise the right conduct in war *(jus in bello)* when the means employed are proportional to the ends sought, when non-combatants are spared, when weapons or other means that are immoral in themselves are not used (typically those that are indiscriminate or cause needless suffering), *and* when actions are taken with a *right intention* to accomplish legitimate military objectives and to minimise collateral death and destruction. Many of these principles of just war are part of the body of international law and, thus, are legally binding on states and their agents [P. Viotti and M. Kauppi, eds., *International Relations Theory* (New York: Macmillan Publishing Company, 1987)].

Legal Positivism

A legal theory that identifies international law with positive acts of state consent. Herein, states are the only official 'subjects' or 'persons' of international law because they have the capacity to enter into legal relations and to have legal rights and duties. Indeed, they are the only entities with full, original and universal legal personality; the only proper actors bound by international law. As far as non-state entities (such as individuals, corporations, and international organisations) are concerned, their ability to assert legal personality is only derivative of, and conditional upon, state personality and state consent. This predominant ideology originated in the 19th century when legal positivism took the 18th century law of nations, a law common to individuals and states, and transformed it into public and private international law, with the former being deemed to apply to states and the latter to individuals. Thus, only states enjoy a full international legal personality, which can be defined as the capacity to bring claims arising from the violation of international law, to conclude valid international agreements, and to enjoy priveleges and immunities from national jurisdiction. [Edited text taken from C. Cutler, "Globalization, Law and Transnational Corporations: a Deepening of Market Discipline", in Cohn, T., S. McBride and J. Wiseman, eds., *Power in the Global Era* (Macmillan Press Ltd., 2000)].

Liberalism (Liberal Internationalism)

Liberalism is a political theory founded on the natural goodness of humans and the autonomy of the individual. It favours civil and political liberties, government by law with the consent of the governed, and protection from arbitrary authority. In international relations, liberalism covers a fairly broad perspective ranging from Wilsonian idealism through to contemporary neo-liberal theories and the democratic peace thesis. Here states are but one actor in world politics, and even states can cooperate together through institutional mechanisms and bargaining that undermine the propensity to base interests simply in military terms. States are interdependent and other actors such as transnational corporations, the International Monetary Fund and the United Nations play a role.

Marxism

A body of thought inspired by Karl Marx. It emphasises the dialectical unfolding of historical stages, the importance of economic and material forces and class analysis. It predicts that contradictions inherent in each historical epoch eventually lead to the rise of a new dominant class. The era of capitalism, according to Marx, is dominated by the bourgeoisie and will give way to a proletarian, or working class, revolution and an era of socialism in which workers own the means of production and move toward a classless, communist society in which the state, historically a tool of the dominant class, will wither away. A number of contemporary theorists have drawn on Marxian insights and categories of analysis—an influence most evident in work on dependency and the world capitalist system [P. Viotti and M. Kauppi, eds., *International Relations Theory* (New York: Macmillan Publishing Company, 1987)].

Materialism

Modernisation Theory

A theory presuming that all countries had similiar starting points and follow similar paths to 'development' along the lines of contemporary 'first-world' societies.

Neo-classical Realism

Neo-conservatism

Neo-liberal Institutionalism

This encompasses those theories which argue that international institutions play an important role in coordinating international cooperation. Proponents begin with the same assumptions used by realists, except for the following: where realists assume that states focus on relative gains and the potential for conflict, neo-liberal institutionalists assume that states concentrate on absolute gains and the prospects for cooperation. Neo-liberal institutionalists believe that the potential for conflict is overstated by realists and suggest that there are countervailing forces, such as repeated interactions, that propel states toward cooperation. They regard cheating as the greatest threat to cooperation and anarchy as the lack of organisation to enforce rules against cheating. Institutions are described by neo-liberals as "persistent and connected sets of rules (formal or informal) that prescribe behavioral roles, constrain activity, and shape expectations" (R. Keohane, "International Institutions: Two Approaches", *International Studies Quarterly,* 32, 1988). Robert Keohane is the scholar most closely identified with neo-liberal institutionalism.

Neo-liberalism

Neo-Marxism

Neo-realism
A theory developed by Kenneth Waltz in which states seek to survive within an anarchical system. Although states may seek survival through power balancing, balancing is not the aim of that behaviour. Balancing is a product of the aim to survive. And because the international system is regarded as anarchic and based on self-help, the most powerful units set the scene of action for others as well as themselves. These major powers are referred to as poles; hence the international system (or a regional subsystem), at a particular point in time, may be characterised as unipolar, bipolar or multipolar.

Neo-traditionalism

New War Theory
Mary Kaldor's new war theory argues that contemporary types of warfare are distinct from the classic modern forms of warfare based on nation-states. New wars are part of a globalised war economy underpinned by transnational ethnicities, globalised arms markets and internationalised Western-global interventions. The new type of warfare is a predatory social condition which damages the economies of neighbouring regions as well as the zone of conflict itself, spreading refugees, identity-based politics and illegal trade. It is also characterised by new forms of violence (the systematic murder of 'others', forced population expulsion and rendering areas uninhabitable) carried out by new militaries (the

decaying remnants of state armies, paramilitary groups, self-defence units, mercenaries and international troops) funded by remittances, diaspora fund-raising, external government assistance and the diversion of international humanitarian aid. Whereas 80 per cent of war victims of the early last century were military personnel, it is estimated that 80 per cent of victims in contemporary wars are civilians. According to Kaldor, this new form of warfare is a political rather than a military challenge, involving the breakdown of legitimacy and the need for a new cosmopolitan politics to reconstruct affected communities and societies. See Mary Kaldor, *New and Old Wars: Organized Violence in a Global Era* (Cambridge, Polity, 1999).

Normative Theory
Normative theory deals precisely with values and value preferences. Unlike empirical theory, however, propositions in normative theory are not subject to empirical test as a means of establishing their truth or falsehood. Normative theory deals not with what *is*, the domain of empirical theory. Rather, normative theory deals explicitly with what *ought* to be—the way the world should be ordered and the value choices decision-makers *should* make [P. Viotti and M. Kauppi, eds., *International Relations Theory*, New York: Macmillan Publishing Company)].

Nuclear Utilisation Theory

Offensive Realism
Offensive realism is a covering term for several theories of international politics and foreign policy that give analytical primacy to the hostile and unforgiving nature of the international system as the cause of conflict. Like defensive realism, some variants of offensive realism build upon, and depart from, Waltz's neo-realism. Offensive realism holds that anarchy (the absence of a worldwide government or universal sovereign) provides strong incentives for expansion. All states strive to maximise their relative power because only the strongest states can guarantee their survival. They pursue expansionist policies when and where the benefits of doing so outweigh the costs. States face the ever-present threat that other states will use force to harm or conquer them. This compels them to improve their relative power positions through arms build-ups, unilateral diplomacy, mercantile (or even autarkic) foreign

economic policies, and opportunistic expansion. Ultimately, every state in the international system strives to become a regional hegemon—a state that enjoys a preponderance of military, economic, and potential power in its part of the globe. Offensive realists, however, disagree over the historical prevalence of hegemonic regional systems and the likely responses of weaker states to would-be regional hegemons (e.g., balancing, buck-passing, or bandwagoning). In particular, there is a sharp disagreement between proponents of the balance-of-power tradition (John Mearsheimer, Eric Labs, Fareed Zakaria, Kier Lieber, and Christopher Layne) and proponents of the security variant of hegemonic stability theory (Robert Gilpin, William Wohlforth, and Stephen Brooks). [Sources: Jeffrey W. Taliaferro, "Security- Seeking Under Anarchy: Defensive Realism Reconsidered," *International Security*, 25, 3, Winter 2000/2001: 152-86; and John J. Mearsheimer, [*Tragedy of Great Power Politics* (New York: W.W. Norton, 2002)].

Parallelism Theory

Based on a fusion of Weberian and Freudian concepts, parallelism argues that, at the macro level, states fall into two general categories, paternal and fraternal, and that the struggle between the two types characterises international relations. In the ancient world, paternal systems were predominant because they were militarily superior, but since the rise of the nation-state, fraternal states have become predominant. The engine of historical change is the revolution-hegemonic war cycle, which brings paternal and fraternal systems into conflict with one another. There are at least four examples of this type of hegemonic conflict occurring in documented history: (1) the rise of Macedonia and Alexander the Great's war with Persia; (2) the rise of Mongolia and Gheghis Khan's war of expansion; (3) the French Revolution and the Napoleonic Wars; and (4) Weimar Germany and World War II. There are other types of hegemonic conflicts (e.g., World War I, Seven Years War), but these four represent parallel events. Victory in revolutionary and hegemonic conflict has determined the direction of the world system, towards paternalism or fraternalism. For more information, refer to the Centre for the Study of Political Parallelism.

Peripheral Realism

Peripheral realism in foreign policy theory arises from the special perspective of (Latin American) peripheral states and represented by the work of Carlos Escude, for example. This view of international relations regards the international system as having an incipient hierarchical structure based on perceived differences among states: those that give orders, those that obey, and those that rebel. The peripheral approach introduces a different way of understanding the international system: that is, from the unique viewpoint of states that do not impose 'rules of the game' and which suffer high costs when they confront them. Thus, the foreign policies of peripheral states are typically framed and implemented in such a way that the national interest is defined in terms of development, confrontation with great powers is avoided, and autonomy is not understood as freedom of action but rather in terms of the costs of using that freedom.

Pluralism

A tradition in international relations that argued that politics, and, hence, policy, pluralism was the product of a myriad competing interests, thereby, depriving the state of any independent status. Pluralism can be seen to derive principally from a liberal tradition, rooted in Locke's "Second Treatise of Government", and to pose an anti-realist vision of the centrality of the state in world politics. Pluralists make four key assumptions about international relations. Primarily, non-state actors are important entities in world politics. Secondly, the state is not looked upon as a unified actor, rather, competition, coalition building, and compromise between various interest groups, including multinational enterprises, will eventually culminate into a 'decision' announced in the name of the state. Thirdly, pluralists challenge the realist assumption of the state as a rational actor, and this derives from the second assumption where the clash of competing interests may not always provide for a rational decision-making process. Finally, the fourth assumption revolves around the nature of the international agenda, where it is deemed extensive by the pluralists and includes issues of national security as well as economic, social and environmental issues. Hence, pluralists reject the 'high politics' 'low politics' divide characteristic of realism. They also contend with the predominance of a physical conception of power inherent in realism.

Policy-Relevant Theory

Policy-relevant theories may have explicit purposes that stem from the value preferences of the theorist, such as reducing the likelihood of war or curbing the arms race. Acting on such theories, of course, is the domain of the policy-maker, a task separate from that of the empirical theorist. Theorists who become policy-makers may well make choices informed by what theories say will be the likely outcomes of implementing one or another alternative. Their choices may be informed by the empirical theory or an understanding of world events, but the decisions they make are still based on value preferences [P. Viotti and M. Kauppi, eds., *International Relations Theory* (New York: Macmillan Publishing Company, 1987)].

Poliheuristic Theory of Foreign Policy Decision-Making
The poliheuristic theory suggests that leaders simplify their choice problems according to a two-stage decision process. During the first stage, the set of possible options and outcomes is reduced by application of a 'noncompensatory principle' to eliminate any alternative with an unacceptable return on a critical, typically political, decision dimension (Mintz, 1993). Once the choice set has been reduced to alternatives that are acceptable to the decision-maker, the process moves to a second stage "during which the decision maker can either use a more analytic, expected utility-like strategy or switch to a lexicographic decision strategy." (Mintz, 1997; Mintz et al., 1997; Mintz and Geva, 1997; Mintz and Astorino-Courtois, 2001). In setting out a pivotal preliminary stage to expected utility decision-making, the poliheuristic theory bridges the gap between research in cognitive psychology (Taber and Steenbergen, 1995) and the considerable insights provided by rational analyses of decision-making (e.g., Bueno de Mesquita, 1981; Bueno de Mesquita and Lalman, 1992; Morrow, 1997). From Mintz, *Integrating Cognitive and Rational Theories of Foreign Policy Decision-Making* (New York: Palgrave Macmillan, 2003).

Positivism

Post-behaviouralism

Post-internationalism
Unlike many other theories, post-international theory is organised around the premise that our time is marked by profound and continuous

transformations and turbulence. It seeks to account for the dynamics of change and anticipate where they might be leading the world. Its prime focus is on the transformation of three basic parameters: one at the micro level of individuals; another at the micro- macro level where individuals and their collectivities interact; and the third is at the macro level of collectivities and their global structures. The central concept at the micro level involves a skill revolution, whereas at the micro-macro level, it involves the pervasiveness of authority crises experienced by all kinds of collectivities; and at the macro level, it posits a bifurcation of global structures into the state-centric world of sovereignty-bound actors and the multi-centric world of sovereignty-free actors. This formulation is theoretical in the sense that it anticipates the conditions under which continual turbulence and transformation are likely to sustain world affairs. Examples of transformations at each level include the increasingly manifest readiness of individuals to engage in collective action (micro level), the 'battle of Seattle' (micro-macro level), and the pattern—indeed, institutionalisation—whereby the Non-Governmental Organisation (NGO) and state-centric worlds converge around common interests (macro level). See James Rosenau's *Turbulence in World Politics* (1990) and Heidi Hobbs', ed., *Pondering Postinternationalism* (2002).

Post-modernism

This is a more extreme branch of critical social theory (see above) that can be identified in terms of its critical stance toward (Western) modernity and the unambiguous narratives of reason, truth and progress. Whereas the dominant narrative of modernity upholds reason as the foundation of objective truth and the source of progress, post-modernism emphasises the interplay of a plurality of discursive practices, ways of knowing, social identities and possible worlds.

Post-positivism

Post-structuralism

Power Transition Theory

Created by A.F.K. Organski and originally published in his textbook, *World Politics* (1958), the power transition theory today describes international politics as a hierarchy with (1) a "dominant" state, the one with the largest proportion of power resources (population, productivity, and political capacity meaning coherence and stability); (2) "great powers," a collection of potential rivals to the dominant state and who share in the tasks of maintaining the system and controlling the allocation of power resources; (3) "middle powers" of regional significance similar to the dominant state, but unable to challenge the dominant state or the system structure; and (4) "small powers," the rest. The principle predictive power of the theory is in the likelihood of war and the stability of alliances. War is most likely, of the longest duration, and greatest magnitude, when a challenger to the dominant power enters into approximate parity with the dominant state and is dissatisfied with the existing system. Similarly, alliances are most stable when the parties to the alliance are satisfied with the system structure. There are further nuances to the theory: for instance, the sources of power transition vary in their volitility, population change being the least volatile and political capacity (defined as the ability of the government to control resources internal to the country) the most volatile. [Best single text and the source of the above description: Ronald L. Tammen et al., *Power Transitions: Strategies for the 21st Century* (Seven Bridges Press, 2000)].

Pragmatic Idealism

Pragmatic idealism was first developed as a conceptual and axiological clarification of "Canadian internationalism" in Costas Melakopides' *Pragmatic Idealism: Canadian Foreign Policy 1945-1995* (McGill-Queens University Press, 1998). It argued that Canada, along with such "like-minded middle powers" as Australia, Denmark, New Zealand, Norway and Sweden, had adopted during the Cold War a self-conscious departure from classic real-politik, through foreign policies that cultivated moderation, mediation, legal and diplomatic solutions to international conflicts, and authentic commitment to peacekeeping, peace-making, human rights, foreign aid, and ecological rationality. Today, pragmatic idealism can be said to characterise any foreign policy—including the international role of the European Union—that embraces the aforementioned principles and values.

Prisoner's Dilemma

Cooperation is usually analysed in game theory by means of a non-zero-sum game called the "Prisoner's Dilemma" (Axelrod, 1984). The two players in the game can choose between two moves, either "cooperate" or "defect". The idea is that each player gains when both cooperate, but if only one of them cooperates, the other one, who defects, will gain more. If both defect, both lose (or gain very little) but not as much as the "cheated" cooperator whose cooperation is not returned. The problem with the prisoner's dilemma is that if both decision-makers were purely rational, they would never cooperate. Indeed, rational decision-making means that you make the decision which is best for you, whatever the other actor chooses. Suppose the other one defects, then it is rational to defect yourself: you won't gain anything, but if you do not defect, you will be stuck with a loss. If the other one cooperates, then you will gain anyway, but you will gain more if you do not cooperate, so here too the rational choice is to defect. The problem is that if both actors are rational, both will decide to defect, and neither of them will gain anything. However, if both "irrationally" decide to cooperate, both will gain.

Prospect Theory

The prospect theory is a psychological theory of decision-making under conditions of risk and derives its name from the tenet that the notion of risk involves some prospect of loss. Thus, the prospect theory posits loss-aversion, rather than risk-aversion (as claimed by rational choice theorists) and takes into account the psychological primacy of relative positioning. The theory states that there are two phases affecting decision-making: (1) framing, where perception or presentation of the situation in which decisions must be made affect the disposition towards some alternatives over others; and (2) evaluation, where the decision-maker assesses gains and losses relative to a movable reference point, depending on the perspective of the decision-maker. It helps focus on how utilities are formed rather than how they are maximised. The prospect theory was originally called 'value theory' by its founders Kahneman and Tversky in the late 1970s. [Edited passages from R. McDermott, ed., *Political Psychology* (Oxford: Blackwell Publishing, 2004)].

Psycho-Cultural Theory

Rationalism

Rationalism is a theoretical qualification to the pessimism of realism and the idealism of liberal internationalism. Rationalists view states as comprising an international *society*, not merely an international system.

States come to be a part of an international society by accepting that various principles and institutions govern the way in which they conduct their foreign relations. In doing so, it can be argued, states also display a commitment to the idea that it is inappropriate to promote the national interest without any regard for international law and morality.

Realism
Realism is a particular view of the world, or paradigm, defined by the following assumptions: the international realm is anarchic and consists of independent political units called states; states are the primary actors and inherently possess some offensive military capability or power which makes them potentially dangerous to each other; states can never be sure about the intentions of other states; the basic motive driving states is survival or the maintenance of sovereignty; states are instrumentally rational and think strategically about how to survive.
Reflectionism

Regime Theory
See International Regime Theory above.

Schema Theory

Securitisation Theory

Security Dilemma
A security dilemma refers to a situation wherein two or more states are drawn into a conflict, possibly even a war, over security concerns, even though none of the states actually desires conflict. Essentially, the security dilemma occurs when two or more states each feel insecure in relation to other states. None of the states involved want relations to deteriorate, let alone for war to be declared, but as each state acts militarily or diplomatically to make itself more secure, the other states interpret its actions as threatening. An ironic cycle of unintended provocations emerges, resulting in an escalation of the conflict which may eventually lead to open warfare. (O. Kanji, "Security" in G. Burgess and H. Burgess, eds., *Beyond Intractability* (Conflict Research Consortium, University of Colorado,2003).

Social Constructivism

Social constructivism is about human consciousness and its role in international life. As such, constructivism rests on an irreducibly inter-subjective dimension of human action: the capacity and will of people to take a deliberate attitude towards the world and to lend it *significance*. This capacity gives rise to social facts, or facts that depend on the human agreement that they exist and typically require human institutions for their existence (money, property rights, sovereignty, marriage and Valentine's Day, for example). Constructivists contend that not only are the identities and interests of actors socially constructed, but also that they must share the stage with a whole host of other ideational factors emanating from people as cultural beings. No general theory of the social construction of reality is available to be borrowed from other fields and international relations constructivists have not as yet managed to formulate a full-fledged theory of their own. As a result, constructivism remains more of a philosophically and theoretically informed perspective on, and approach to, the empirical study of international relations. (Edited passage from J. Ruggie, "What Makes the World Hang Together? Neo-utilitarianism and the Social Constructivist Challenge", *International Organization* 52, 4, Autumn 1998).

State Cartel Theory

The state cartel theory is an institutionalist approach, with a focus on regional integration. It imports its terminology from the classical cartel theory of economic enterprises. Realising that the benefits of cooperation most often outweigh the costs of conflict, states are willing to cartelise political issues in international institutions. A members' assembly is the primary institution, with further organisations being an expression of the will and needs of members. A good example is the Council of the European Union and its allied European Commission and European Court.

Structural Idealism

Structuralism

Supranationalism

Traditionalism

An approach to international relations that emphasises the study of such disciplines as diplomatic history, international law, and philosophy in an attempt to develop better insights. Traditionalists tend to be sceptical of the behaviouralist approaches that are confined to strict scientific standards that include formal hypothesis testing and, usually, the use of statistical analysis [P. Viotti and M. Kauppi, eds., *International Relations Theory* (New York: Macmillan Publishing Company, 1987)].

Transnational Historical Materialism

Transnational historical materialism falls within the Marxist tradition. This contemporary Marxism takes its inspiration from Antonio Gramsci and gives greater significance to the role of culture and ideas, along with focussing on the economic aspects of order and change. It is seen as a corrective to the economism of classical Marxism.

Transnationalism

This comprises interactions and coalitions across state boundaries that involve such diverse non-governmental actors as multinational corporations and banks, church groups, and terrorist networks. In some usages, transnationalism includes both non-governmental as well as *transgovernmental* links. The term *transnational* is used to label both the actor (for example, a transnational actor) or a pattern of behaviour (for example, ·an international organisation that acts *transnationally* - operates across state borders). Theorists focussing on transnationalism often deemphasise the state as the primary and unitary actor [P. Viotti and M. Kauppi, eds., *International Relations Theory* (New York: Macmillan Publishing Company, 1987)].

Two-World Order

Virtual Theory

World Capitalist System

An approach to international relations that emphasises the impact of the worldwide spread of capitalism. It focusses on class and economic relations and the division of the world into a dominant centre or core of industrialised countries, a subordinate periphery of less developed countries and a semi-periphery of countries that occupy an intermediate position between the core and periphery [P. Viotti and M. Kauppi, eds., *International Relations Theory* (New York: Macmillan Publishing Company, 1987)].

World-Systems Analysis

World-systems analysis is not a theory or mode of theorising, but a perspective and a critique of other perspectives within social science. Its social origins were located in the geopolitical emergence of the Third World in the late 1960s and the manifest in the insufficiencies of modernisation theory to account for what is happening. The unit of analysis is the world-system rather than a state or society, with particular emphasis on the long-term history and totality of the system. The notion of totality (globality, unidisciplinarity and holism) distinguishes world-systems analysis from similar approaches such as global or international political economy which look at the relationships between the two segregated streams of politics and economics. Proponents of world-systems analysis also regard it as an intellectual *movement*, capable of transforming social science into a vehicle for worldwide social change.

APPENDIX - B

Nuclear Proliferation

Thérès e Delpech, Nuclear Deterrence in the 21st century, Published 2012 by the RAND Corporation, pp.1-7

The book:
- spells out the need for revitalisation of thinking about nuclear weapons, a challenge that has to be undertaken;
- reviews the key concepts of past deterrence thinking and their development up to now;
- reviews today's key security challenges and their relation to nuclear weapons;
- demonstrates that some of the concepts of the past remain relevant today;
- urges the new generation of defence and security analysts to turn its attention to nuclear deterrence, much as she did 30 years ago.

The INTRODUCTION is an excellent preview of the history of nuclear proliferation and nuclear deterrence. It forms the backdrop to understand nuclear proliferation that has taken place today in North Korea and, hence, should serve as a framework of analysis of nuclear proliferation today.

Introduction

Andrei Antonovich, are you sure this is just an exercise?

—Leonid Brezhnev to Marshal Andrei Grechko
during a 1972 nuclear exercise[1]

There is nothing more difficult to take in hand, more perilous to conduct, or more uncertain in its success, than to take the lead in the conduct of a new order of things.

—Niccolo Machiavelli[2]

This book recommends a renewed intellectual effort on nuclear deterrence. The reasons, spelled out in Chapter Two, are many, but the core principle is straightforward.

As long as nuclear weapons are around, even in small numbers, deterrence is the safest doctrine to deal with them.[3] This principle is easier to embrace in theory than it is to put into practice. This was true during the Cold War, and it appears to be even truer today: The actors are more diverse, more opaque, and sometimes more reckless. Since deterrence is a dynamic relationship among specific entities, nations, and leaders, this diversity, opacity, and potential recklessness must be taken into account. In some cases, this is a real challenge. For example, if Iran ever became a nuclear power, it is difficult even to guess who the interlocutor would be if a serious crisis were to erupt. Traditional nuclear concepts (i.e., first strike, escalation, and extended deterrence), presented in Chapter Three, are often still useful, but they need to be adapted. Finally, unlike all the leaders of the Cold War, today's leaders have not had the experience of living through a major war. The effort to contain violence and prevent escalation is a daily exercise. Leaders must be prepared to respond quickly and decisively in a crisis.

Lessons from past nuclear crises are numerous, including crises in Asia, the proclaimed centre of strategic affairs in the 21st century (Chapter Four). At the moment, we live in a world where a few small states with highly destructive capabilities have acquired the ability to present strategic challenges to major nations. They benefit from the rapid spread of technology as well as from irresponsible past or present military— or dual-use—international cooperation (Chapter Five). But confrontation among big states with widely different approaches to law, stability, and use of force may come back within some decades. This possibility may seem remote, but it is already visible on the horizon (Chapter Six). This time, new domains such as space and cyber space will be part of the battle. In some ways, this battle has already begun: in cyber space, for example, attacks are now taking place on a daily basis in peacetime, mainly for espionage purposes. These domains pose difficult challenges to deterrence (attribution, for example) and they require new thinking (Chapter Seven).

The absence of a chapter on nuclear terrorism, listed as the first threat in the 2010 U.S. Nuclear Posture Review (NPR), might seem surprising to an American audience.

There are two reasons for this omission: first, a number of excellent American analyses on the subject have been published in recent years, and little can be added to them; second, the author tends to agree with Brian Jenkins, who wrote in 2008 that "it is hard to separate truth from myth" in this domain, and that "a world of fantasies, nightmares, hoaxes, scams and stings" is not backed by evidence or historical records.[4] This is not to say that complacency is warranted, but that the anticipation of nuclear terrorism should not have such a high degree of priority and should not drive American defence or nuclear policy. This is also true for Europe, where a British intelligence report leaked to the press in 2007 predicted a large-scale nuclear attack by al Qaeda operatives "on par with Hiroshima and Nagasaki."[5] Sometimes, we succeed in terrorising ourselves. Other nuclear realities look more troubling to this author are: China's unabated nuclear and ballistic missile modernisation, its lack of transparency on issues of command and control, and the fact that a confrontation over Taiwan or over the South China Sea would pose the most serious danger of nuclear war since 1962; Russia's nuclear doctrine (overt and covert[6]) coupled with military exercises rehearsing the use of nuclear weapons against separatist forces (the 2010 Vostok manoeuvres) and Moscow's suspected continuous violation of the Biological Weapons Convention (BWC);[7] Pakistan's perceived recklessness and its apparent inability to deal with the potentially mortal threat of extremism; progress in the nuclear and ballistic missile programmes of both Iran and North Korea, two non-status-quo nations; the number of countries that will potentially be operating nuclear reactors by 2030;[8] and, last but not least, the lack of sustained thinking on the new conditions under which nuclear weapons might operate in the 21st century.

Are nuclear weapons, while less central, becoming more dangerous? According to the Global Trends 2025 report, "The risk of nuclear weapon use over the next 20 years, although remaining very low, is likely to be greater than it is today."[9] The report presents the consequences of any nuclear weapon use: if nuclear weapons are used in the next 15–20 years, the international system will be shocked as it experiences immediate humanitarian, economic and political-military repercussions. A future use of nuclear weapons would probably bring about significant geopolitical changes as some states would seek to establish or reinforce security alliances with existing nuclear powers and others would push for global nuclear disarmament.[10]

There are now seven overt nuclear powers, one covert nuclear power (Israel), and at least three nuclear aspirants (Iran, North Korea, and Syria), making the nuclear phenomenon more global than ever. New nuclear players may still emerge in the next decades in East Asia, the Middle East, or South Asia. As of 2010, at least 25 states had announced their desire to build nuclear reactors before 2030, which could have major implications for regional and international security if it leads to further nuclear proliferation. In all the regions mentioned above, conditions exist that make nuclear weapons more hazardous and increase the risk of use: the recurrence of armed conflicts since 1945, the severity of tensions, and the absence of a recognised status quo regarding borders (such as the India–Pakistan and India–China borders), territories (non-recognition of Israel by most nations in the Middle East), and peace treaties (China and the Korean Peninsula). Although it is difficult to predict the behaviour of any actor in times of serious crises, it is even more difficult to do so in the case of these new actors, notably because our knowledge concerning them is so poor.

During the Cold War, the United States had two overriding objectives: to avoid all-out war with the Soviet Union and to prevent Soviet political and territorial gains.

Both sides proved—most of the time at least—to be cautious and even frightened by the mere possibility of a nuclear exchange, as Brezhnev's epigraph illustrates. The central issue was the preservation of an order acknowledged by both sides, something that does not exist in the Middle East, South Asia, or East Asia today. As a result, the traditional goal of preserving the status quo—reportedly the most important role of nuclear weapons during the Cold War—does not apply, because it goes against the wishes of those who would like to challenge the regional or international order.

In addition, the evolving relationship between the United States and China is more likely to be vexed than cooperative, not only on exchange rates and trade, but on security issues—notably on Taiwan and the South China Sea, the issue capable of starting a nuclear conflict among major actors in this century. Although the aims of China's ballistic missile and nuclear modernisation are not known, the fact that China is the only nuclear weapon state building up its arsenal is now frequently underlined. How exactly will this arsenal evolve? How will the relationship between the Chinese Communist Party (CCP) and the People's Liberation Army (PLA) evolve? This question depends heavily on the political evolution in Beijing. How will China's nuclear capabilities be coupled with its conventional means? Will China follow in practice the prudent nuclear policy that it proclaims? These are difficult and decisive questions for regional and international security, with implications for India and Pakistan, and also globally. Recent years show a clear deterioration of China's relationship with the West, and even Moscow recognises behind closed doors that its relationship with Beijing is "complex."[11]

For decades, almost every American administration has come into office vowing to get tougher with China, only to soften its approach after a while. The Obama Administration adopted the opposite approach, starting with cooperative offers only to realise later that Beijing shows little intention of working with Washington.[12] One reason for China's recalcitrance is the conclusion drawn in Beijing after the 2008 economic crisis.

China's fast rebound has led it to believe that the United States is a declining power while China is a rising power. In October 2010, Washington— which, three months earlier in Hanoi, had been able to line up 12 countries of the region behind its position concerning the South China Sea—made it clear to Beijing that it has closer and deeper friendships elsewhere in the region. This also means that pressure for the extension of a US security umbrella has increased in East Asia as much as it has in the Middle East, where Iran's regional policy is worrying its neighbours.

Extended deterrence will be needed to protect US allies from China's increasingly tough policy, notably regarding sea lanes and maritime disputes. The key question for the two decades to come will be whether the United States is up to the task, particularly if China openly ceases to be a status quo power. With this in mind, those engaged in day-to-day dealings with China would do well to recall one of the most important assertions made by Thomas Schelling concerning reputation: "Face," Schelling wrote, is not "a frivolous asset to preserve" but "one of the few things worth fighting over," not only because it preserves credibility and, therefore, secures extended deterrence, but also because it prevents dangerous future contingencies from happening.[13]

The notion of a second nuclear age emerged in the late 1990s.[14] It may be taken as having a number of meanings. At its most basic, it can be understood as a simple acknowledgment that the end of the Cold War did not mean the end of nuclear weapons, either because the nuclear shadow of the past 50 years proved to be more consequential than it was assumed to be in 1989, or because more countries are taking an interest in those weapons. The term second nuclear age can also mean that the new era is not bound by the rules of the old one. The relationship between nuclear and conventional weapons is evolving rapidly, and new forms of deterrence are appearing, including those involving the offence–defence balance. Various combinations of offensive and defensive means are already surfacing. Third, a second nuclear age can refer to the advent of new nuclear powers. Such states (or, in the future, non-state actors) are dissatisfied with a regional or international order that they regard as inappropriate.

Nuclear weapons could be instrumental in changing that order, through coercion, threats, effective use, or simply possession. In any case, the risk of use rises with the number and diversity of players for whom, in addition, deterrence could have different meanings. Fifty years of non-use have not enshrined a policy of deterrence, nor a nuclear taboo. Last, a second nuclear age means that security in the 21st century is, to a large extent, determined by events in Asia. Those wishing to exert influence on the international scene will have to understand developments there.

In the West, there is continued marginalisation and restriction of the role of nuclear weapons, while in Asia—from West Asia to East Asia—a threat to the preservation of nuclear peace in the 21st century can be observed. The problem is less about the number of weapons—although countries in the region are increasing their nuclear arsenals—than about the number of players and the long history of tensions among them, about cultural differences that could exacerbate misunderstandings, and about the weakness of regional and global regulatory mechanisms. Finally, today's leaders may be ill-prepared to handle crises involving non-conventional weapons, particularly nuclear weapons.

In terms of stability, the goal should not be to restore an order that has disappeared (assuming that strategic stability ever did exist during the Cold War) but to look for forms of stability that are relevant in this century. A "multipolar world" of the future[15] is likely to be more unstable than a bipolar or—contrary to anti-American or anti-Western opinion—unipolar world. Such a world is just as likely to be one of confrontation as of stability, as the European experience of the last three centuries has shown.[16] Extending the nuclear peace the world has known for 50 years would involve both reducing the likelihood of conflict in zones where nuclear weapons exist (these are inherently volatile zones) and making crisis escalation unlikely in the event of such conflicts (since today's actors may be more risk-prone than Cold War warriors). The task is not going to be easy, not only because of potential volatility and recklessness but also because of the mounting violence worldwide and the absence of recognised rules. As Machiavelli remarked, there is nothing more difficult, perilous, and uncertain than "to take the lead in the conduct of a new order of things."[17]

How is this "new order of things" to be described? In a nutshell, the West's potential adversaries understand the meaning of conventional superiority for future conflicts: They already employ a mix of conventional weapons, irregular tactics, anti-access capabilities, space and cyber space weapons, terrorism, and criminal behaviour to further their objectives. Even a surprise nuclear attack, the major fear of the Cold War, may become more likely *inter alia* because of the West's perceived conventional superiority.[18]

More than ever before, no one can assume that every action in a crisis will follow a finely calculated plan. Put another way, an era of strategic piracy may be opening up, where piracy is defined as lawlessness and deception. Traditional actors are ill-prepared for it. The new faces of nuclear doctrines and the difficulty of maintaining efficient deterrence strategies are integral parts of the new era. They just might be the most dangerous side of it. A renewed intellectual effort is, therefore, warranted. The RAND Corporation is the best place for it to start.

Notes

1. John G. Hines, Ellis M. Mishulovich, and John F. Shull, Soviet Intentions 1965–1985, Vol II, *Soviet Post- Cold War Testimonial Evidence* (McLean, Va.: BDM Federal, Inc., September 22, 1995), p. 27.
2. Niccolo Machiavelli, *The Prince*.
3. Alternatives to deterrence—preemption, coercion, and use—are all less attractive. Deterrence matters most to nations willing to limit violence escalation. It follows, then, that deterrence matters most to risk-averse democracies, whether they be Western, Asian, or Middle Eastern. It took some time for the Western nations to convince Moscow that deterrence was the best policy when nuclear weapons were involved. It remains unclear today whether that attempt was fully successful. In the case of China, deterrence, for long, meant coercion, and may still mean it behind closed doors. How Pakistan, Iran, and North Korea calculate prospective costs and benefits remains an enigma.

4. Brian Michael Jenkins, *Will Terrorists Go Nuclear?* (Amherst, N.Y.: Prometheus Books, 2008).

5. Dipesh Gadher, "Al Qaeda 'Planning Big British Attack'," *The Sunday Times*, April 22, 2007, p. 10. The intelligence report, produced in early April 2007, was compiled by the Joint Terrorism Analysis Centre (JTAC), based at the MI5's London headquarters.

6. The Russian nuclear doctrine published in 2010, reflects a series of internal debates following the comments of Nikolai Patrushev, Secretary of the Security Council, who reportedly explained that delays in completing the new military doctrine were due to discussions concerning the right of "preventive nuclear strikes" (RIA Novosti, "Russia's New Military Doctrine Allows Pre-Emptive Nuclear Strikes," October 14, 2009). The remark followed a simulated nuclear strike on Polish soil during the Zapad 2009 exercise. The nature of a political system in a nuclear state has an impact on doctrine projection and, sometimes, on the opacity shrouding it.

7. The size of the Soviet offensive biological empire between 1972 and 1992 makes Russia's suspected continuous violation of the BWC a major international issue. Violations of the Conventional Armed Forces in Europe (CFE) Treaty (on flanks and ceilings), the former Start I Treaty [reportedly violated until it ended), and the 1987 Intermediate Nuclear Forces (INF) Treaty (at 700 km, the range of the Russian ballistic missile Iskander-M is much greater than advertised, according to the Finnish security expert Stefan Forss (unpublished conference presentation, Helsinki, Finland, September 2010)], while less troubling than the violation of the BWC if confirmed, nonetheless indicate a disturbing pattern of Russian noncompliance.

8. The Fukushima nuclear accident has likely led to revisions in some of these projects, particularly in nations where the safety record of nuclear power is still poor.

9. National Intelligence Council, *Global Trends 2025: A Transformed World*, (Washington, D.C.: U.S. Government Printing Office, November 2008), p. 10.

10. Ibid., p. 10.

11. This was reportedly the word used by Russian President Dmitry Medvedev when he met with French President Nicolas Sarkozy and German Chancellor Angela Merkel in Deauville, France, on October 19, 2010. Off-the record interview with French officials, October 2010.

12. According to David Shambaugh, Director of the China policy programme at George Washington University, "This administration came in with one dominant idea: make China a global partner in facing global challenges. China failed to step up and play that role. Now, they realize they are dealing with an increasingly narrow-minded, self-interested, truculent, hyper-nationalist and powerful country." Mark Landler and Sewell Chan, "Taking Harder Stance Toward China, Obama Lines Up Allies," *New York Times*, October 25, 2010.

13. Thomas Schelling, *Arms and Influence* (New Haven, Conn.: Yale University Press, 1966), p. 124.

14. Keith Payne, *Deterrence in the Second Nuclear Age* (Lexington: University Press of Kentucky, 1996); Thérèse Delpech, "Nuclear Weapons and the 'New World Order': Early Warning from Asia?," *Survival*, Vol. 40, No. 4, 1999; Paul Bracken, *Fire in the East: The Rise of Asian Military Power and the Second Nuclear Age* (New York: HarperCollins, 1999); and Colin Gray, *The Second Nuclear Age* (London: Lynn Rienner Publishers).

15. See Eric Edelman, "Understanding America's Contested Primacy," Centre for Strategic and Budgetary Assessments, Fall 2010, p. 67: "Whether the international system moves toward a multipolar world, as forecast by Global Trends 2025, however, will depend to a large degree on how people perceive the relative shifts in power and how they choose to act on those perceptions."

16. This does not mean that confrontation and stability should be considered mutually exclusive but rather that proponents of multi-polarity believe— wrongly, in the author's view—that the concept suggests stability, when in fact, the poles are equally likely to clash, perhaps even violently.

17. Machiavelli, n. 2.

18. The Chinese concept of "deescalatory strikes," for example, is worrisome.

APPENDIX – C

Suggested Further Reading

I. Books and Booklets

1. Jean-Marc F. Blanchard, Edward D. Mansfield, and Norrin M. Ripsman, eds., *Power and the Purse: Economic Statecraft, Interdependence, and National Security* (London: Frank Cass, 1999). Originally published as a special issue of Security Studies 9.1-2, Autumn 1999 – Winter 2000, pp. 1-316.

2. William Ernest Blatz, *Human Security: Some Reflections* (London: University of London Press, 1967).

3. Barry Buzan, Ole Wæver, and Jaap de Wilde, *Security: A New Framework for Analysis* (Boulder: Lynne Rienner, 1998).

4. David Campbell, *Writing Security: United States Foreign Policy and the Politics of Identity* (Manchester: Manchester University Press, 1998).

5. Edward Clay, and Olav Stokke, *Food Aid and Human Security* (London: Frank Cass Publishers, 2000).

6. Chris Cocklin, and Steve Lonergan, eds., *Water and Human Security in Southeast Asia and Oceania*. Papers presented at the workshop on Water and Human Security in Southeast Asia and Oceania, co-sponsored by GECHS and HDP Australia, Canberra, Australia, November 16-18, 1998. Forthcoming.

7. Tony Evans and Caroline Thomas, *The Politics of Human Rights: A Global Perspective Human Security in the Global Economy* (Pluto Press, 2001).

8. Graduate Institute of International Studies, *Small Arms Survey 2001: Profiling the Problem* (Oxford: Oxford University Press, April 26, 2001).

9. David T Graham and Nana K. Poku, eds., *Migration, Globalization and Human Security* (London: Routledge Research in Population and Migration, 2000).

10. Arthur C Helton, *Forced Displacement and Human Security in the Former Soviet Union: Law and Policy* (Transnational Publishers, July 2000).

11. Thomas Homer-Dixon and Jessica Blitt, eds., *Ecoviolence: Links Among Environment, Population, and Security* (Lanham, MD: Rowman & Littlefield Publishers, Inc., 1999).

12. Human Development Centre, *Human Development in South Asia 1999: The Crisis of Governance* (Karachi: Oxford University Press, 1999).

13. Robert Jackson, *The Global Covenant: Human Conduct in a World of States* (Oxford: Oxford University Press, 2000).

14. Richard Wyn Jones, *Security, Strategy, and Critical Theory* (Boulder, CO: Lynne Rienner, 1999).

15. Inge Kaul, Isabelle Grunberg and Marc A. Stern, *Global Public Goods: International Cooperation in the Twenty-first Century* (New York: Oxford University Press, 1999).

16. Cristóbal Kay, ed., *Globalisation, Competitiveness and Human Security* (London: Frank Cass and Company Limited, 1997).

17. Uner Kirdar and Leonard Silk, eds., *People: From Impoverishment to Empowerment* (New York: NYU Press, 1995).

18. Jeni Klugman, *Social and Economic Policies to Prevent Complex Humanitarian Emergencies* (Washington DC: United Nations University World Institute for Development Economics Research, 1999).

19. Keith Krause and Michael C. Williams, eds., *Critical Security Studies: Concepts and Cases* (London: UCL Press, 1997).

20. David Lake and Donald Rothchild, eds., *The International Spread of Ethnic Conflict: Fear, Diffusion, and Escalation* (Princeton, NJ: Princeton University Press, 1998), p. 21. Ellen Lammers, *Refugees, Gender and Human Security: A Theoretical Introduction and Annotated Bibliography* (Utrecht: International Books, 1999).

22. Stephen C Lonergan, Aaron Wolf and Chris Cocklin, eds., *Water and Human Security in Southeast Asia* (Tokyo: UNU Press, Forthcoming 2002).

23. Stephen C Lonergan, ed., *Environmental Change, Adaptation and Security*. Proceedings of the NATO Advanced Research Workshop, held in Budapest, Hungary, from October 16-18, 1997 (Dordrecht: Kluwer Academic Publishers, 1999).

24. Sean M Lynn-Jones and Steven E Miller, eds., *Global Dangers: Changing Dimensions of International Security* (Cambridge, MA: MIT Press, 1995).

25. Tatsuro Matsumae and Lincoln C Chen, eds., *Common Security in Asia – New Concepts in Human Security* (Tokyo: Tokai University Press, 1995).

26. Rob McRae and Don Hubert, eds., *Human Security and the New Diplomacy: Protecting People, Promoting Peace* (Montreal: McGill-Queen's University Press, 2001).

27. Bill McSweeney, *Security, Identity, and Interests: A Sociology of International Relations* (Cambridge: Cambridge University Press, 1999).

28. Patricia Mische and Gerald, *Toward a Human World Order: Beyond the National Security Straitjacket* (New York: Paulist Press, 1977).

29. Jorge Nef, *Human Security and Mutual Vulnerability*, 2nd edition (Canada: International Research Development Centre, 1999), http://www.idrc.ca/books/focus/879/index.html, August 22, 2001.

30. Joan M Nelson, *Poverty, Inequality, and Conflict in Developing Countries* (New York: Rockefeller Brothers Fund, Inc., 1998), http://www.rbf.org/pws/poverty.pdf, August 27, 2001

31. Amir Pasic, *Culture, Identity, and Security: An Overview* (New York: Rockefeller Brothers Fund, Inc., 1998), http://www.rbf.org/pws/Pasic_Culture_Identity.pdf, August 27, 2001.

32. Nana K Poku and David T Graham, eds., *Redefining Security: Population Movements and National Security* (Westport, CT: Praeger, 1998).

33. Michael Renner, *Fighting for Survival: Environmental Decline, Social Conflict and the New Age of Insecurity* (Washington, DC: Worldwatch Institute, 1996.

34. Thomas Risse, Stephen C Ropp and Kathryn Sikkink, eds., *The Power of Human Rights: International Norms and Domestic Change* (New York: Cambridge University Press, 1999).

35. Stephen John Stedman, *International Actors and Internal Conflicts* (New York: Rockefeller Brothers Fund, Inc., 1999), http://www.rbf.org/publications_security.html, August 20, 2001.

36. Peter Stoett, *Human and Global Security: An Exploration of Terms* (Toronto: University of Toronto Press, 1999).

37. Majid Tehranian, ed., *Asian Peace: Security and Governance in the Asia Pacific Region*, Human Security and Global Governance Series (New York: I.B. Tauris, 1999).

38. Majid Tehranian, ed., *Worlds Apart: Human Security and Global Governance*, in association with the Toda Institute for Global Peace and Policy Research (London: I.B. Tauris, 1999).

39. Ramesh Thakur and Edward Newman, eds., *New Millennium, New Perspectives, the United Nations, Security, and Governance*, UNU Millennium Series (Tokyo: United Nations University Press, 2000).

40. Caroline Thomas and Peter Wilkin, eds., *Globalization, Human Security, and the African Experience* (Boulder/London: Lynne Rienner Publishers, Inc., 1999).

41. Caroline Thomas, *Global Governance, Development and Human Security: The Challenge of Poverty and Inequality* (London: Pluto Press, 2000).

42. William T Tow, Ramesh Thakur and In-Taek Hyun, eds., *Asia's Emerging Regional Order: Reconciling Traditional and Human Security* (Tokyo: United Nations University Press, 2000), http://ciaonet.org/book/tow, August 22, 2001.

43. Nicolas Van de Walle, *Economic Globalization and Political Stability in Developing Countries* (New York: Rockefeller Brothers Fund, Inc., 1998), http://www.rbf.org/pws/globalization.pdf, August 27, 2001.

44. Heloise Weber and Caroline Thomas, eds., *The Politics of Microcredit: Global Governance and Poverty Reduction, Human Security in the Global Economy* (Pluto Press, 2000).

45. Agostinho Zacarias, *Security and the State in Southern Africa* (London: I.B. Tauris Publishers, 1999).

II. Chapters in Books

1. "Proceedings of the 28th Annual Conference of the Canadian Council on International Law, Ottawa, October 28-29, 1999," *From Territorial Sovereignty to Human Security/De la souveraineté territoriale à la sécurité humaine,* ed. *Canadian Council on International Law/Conseil canadien de droit international* (The Hague: Kluwer Law International, November 2000).

2. Dayle Bethel, "An Asian Philosophy of Peace and Human Security," in Majid Tehranian, ed., *Asian Peace Security and Governance in the Asia Pacific Region* (London: I.B. Tauris Publishers London), pp. 173-185, in association with the Toda Institute for Global Peace and Policy Research, 1999.

3. Barry Buzan, "Human Security in International Perspective," in Mely C Anthony and Mohamed Jawhar Hassan, eds., *The Asia Pacific in the New Millenium: Political and Security Challenges* (Kuala Lumpur, Malaysia: ISIS Malaysia), pp. 583-596.

4. John G Cockell, "Conceptualising Peacebuilding: Human Security and Sustainable Peace," in Michael Pugh, ed., *Regeneration of War-Torn Societies* (London: Macmillan, 2000).

5. Simon Dalby, "Threats from the South? Geopolitics, Equity, and Environmental Security," in D Deudney and Richard M Matthew, *Contested Grounds: Security and Conflict in the New Environmental Politics* (Albany, NY: State University of New York Press), pp. 155-185.

6. Mark Gwozdecky and John Sinclair, "Case Study: Landmines and Human Security," in Rob McRae and Don Hubert, eds., *Human Security and the New Diplomacy* (Montreal: McGill- Queen's University Press, 2001), pp. 28-40.

7. Stuart Harris and Andrew Mack, "Security and Economics in East Asia," in Stuart Harris and Andrew Mack, eds., *Asia–Pacific Security: The Economics–Politics Nexus* (Sydney), pp. 1-29.

Journal and Magazine Articles

1. M C Abad Jr, "The Challenge of Balancing State Security with Human Security," *Indonesian Quarterly,* XXVII.4, 2000, pp. 403-410.

2. Itty Abraham, "Nuclear Power and Human Security," *Bulletin of Concerned Asian Scholars,* 31.2, 1999.

3. Arabinda Acharya and Amitav Acharya, "Human Security in the Asia Pacific: Puzzle, Panacea, or Peril?," *CANCAPS Bulletin du CONCSAP* No. 27, November 2000, http://www.iir.ubc.ca/cancaps/cbul27.html#husec, August 22, 2001.

4. Kofi Annan, "Human Security and Intervention," Vital Speeches of the Day 66.1, 1999.

5. Oscar Arias, "Economics and Disarmament After the Cold War – Human Security: Our Common Responsibility," *Disarmament: A Periodic Review* by the UN 19.3, 1996, pp. 7-17.

6. Oscar Arias Sanchez, "Human Security: Our Common Responsibility." *Disarmament: A Periodic Review,* 19.3, 1996.

7. Juha Auvinen and Wayne E Nafziger, "The Sources of Humanitarian Emergencies," *Journal of Conflict Resolution,* 43.3, 1999, pp. 267-290.

8. Lloyd Axworthy, "Human Security and Global Governance: Putting People First," *Global Governance*, 2001, pp. 19-23.

9. Lloyd Axworthy, "NATO's New Security Vocation," *NATO Review*, 47.2, 1999, pp. 8-11.

10. Lloyd Axworthy, "Canada and Human Security: The Need for Leadership," *International Journal*, 52.2, 1997, pp.183-196.

11. William W Bain, "Against Crusading: The Ethic of Human Security and CFP," *Canadian Foreign Policy*, 6.3, Spring 1999, pp. 85-98.

12. William Bain, "The Tyranny of Benevolence: National Security, Human Security, and the Practice of Statecraft," *Global Society*, 15.3, July 2001.

13. Kanti Bajpai, "The Idea of a Human Security Audit," *Report 19*, 2000, pp. 1-4, http://www.nd.edu/~krocinst/report/report19/lead.html, August 22, 2001.

14. David A Baldwin, "Security Studies and the End of the Cold War," *World Politics*, 48.1, 1995, pp. 117-141.

15. David A Baldwin, "The Concept of Security," *Review of International Studies*, 23.1, January 1997, pp. 5-26.

16. Bertram Bastiampillai, "Role of Human Security in Regional Security and Peace in South Asia," *Regional Studies*, 16.4, 1998.

17. Mart T Berger, "The United Nations, Regional Organizations and Human Security: Building Theory in Central America," *Third World Quarterly*, 15.2, 1994.

18. Richard K Betts, "Should Security Studies Survive?," *World Politics*, 50.1 1997, pp. 7-33, http://muse.jhu.edu/journals/wp/, August 8, 2001.

19. Manfred F Boemeke, "The Changing Face of Peace: New Security Challenges and the United Nations," *Work in Progress*, A Review of Research Activities of the United Nations University, 15.3, Summer 1999, http://www.unu.edu/hq/ginfo/wip/wip-sum99.html, August 28, 2001.

20. Leen Boer and Ad Koekkoek, "Development and Human Security," *Third World Quarterly*, 15.3, 1994, pp. 519-522.

21. Paz Buttedahl, "Viewpoint: True Measures of Human Security," *IRDC Reports*, 22.3, October 1994, pp. 1-5, http://www.idrc.ca/books/reports/V223/view.html, August 8, 2001.

22. Mely Caballero-Anthony, "Human Security (and) Comprehensive Security in ASEAN," *Indonesian Quarterly*, XXVII.4, 2000, pp. 413-422.

23. Sharon Capeling-Alakija, "Shared Vision: Women and Global Human Security," *Development 2*, 1994, pp. 44-48.

24. Lincoln C Chen and Aafje Rietveld, "Human Security During Complex Humanitarian Emergencies: Rapid Assessment and Institutional Capabilities," *Medicine and Global Survival*, 1.3, 1994.

25. Erskine Childers, "New Ethics for a Global World," *Development 2*, 1994, pp. 49-50.

26. Steven J Del Rosso Jr, "The Insecure State: Reflections on 'The State' and 'Security' in a Changing World," *Daedalus: Journal of the American Academic of Arts and Sciences*, 124.2, 1995, p. 175, http://www.mtholyoke.edu/acad/intrel/rosso.htm, August 22, 2001.

27. Daniel Deudney, "Environment and Security: Muddled Thinking," *Bulletin of the Atomic Scientists*, 47.3, 1991, p. 23.

28. A Walter Dorn, "Small Arms, Human Security and Development," *Development Express*, 5, 1999-2000, http://www.acdicida.gc.ca/cida_ind.nsf/8949395286e4d3a58525641300568be1/6f5d62d208f5339585256a4a00004?OpenDocument, August 9, 2001.

29. Xavier Furtado, "Human Security and Asia's Financial Crisis: A Critique of Canadian Policy," *International Journal*, 55.3, 2000.

30. Keith Griffin, "Global Prospects for Development and Human Security," *Canadian Journal of Development Studies*, 16.3, 1995, pp. 359-370.

31. H Hafterdorn, "The Security Puzzle: Theory-Building and Discipline-Building in International Security," *International Studies Quarterly*, 35.1, March 1991, pp. 3-17.

32. Anne Hammerstad, "Whose Security? UNHCR, Refugee Protection and State Security After the Cold War," *Security Dialogue*, 31.4, 2000, pp. 391-403.

33. Fen Osler Hampson and Dean F Oliver, "Pulpit Diplomacy: A Critical Assessment of the Axworthy Doctrine," *International Journal*, LIII.3, 1998, pp. 379-406.

34. Mahbub ul-Haq, "Human Rights, Security, and Governance," *Peace & Policy Journal* of the Toda Institute for Global Peace and Policy Research 3.2, Fall/Winter 1998, http://www.toda.org/publications/peace_policy/p_p_fw98/haq.html, August 9, 2001.

35. Mahbub ul-Haq, "New Imperatives of Human Security: Barbara Ward Lecture, 1972," *Development 2*, 1994, pp. 40-43.

36. Paul Heinbecker, "Human Security," *Canadian Foreign Policy*, 7.1, 1999, pp. 19-25.

37. Paul Heinbecker, "Human Security: The Hard Edge," *Canadian Military Journal*, 1.1, Spring 2000, http://www.journal.dnd.ca/vol1/no1_e/policy_e/pol1_e.html, August 8, 2001.

38. Inge Kaul, "Guest Editorial – A New Ethic of Global Human Security," *Development 3*, 1995.

39. Inge Kaul, "Peace Needs No Weapons: From Military Security to Human Security," *The Ecumenical Review*, 47.3, 1995.

40. Yuen Foong Khong, "Human Security: A Shotgun Approach to Alleviating Human Misery?," *Global Governance*, 2001, Forthcoming.

41. David Kilgour, "Reconsidering Sovereignty: The UN and the Challenge of Human Security," *McGill International Review*, 1.1, Winter 2000, http://www.unsam.qc.ca/mir/issue1/features4.htm, August 28, 2001.

42. David Kilgour, "The Front Line: Giving the UN a Human Security Focus," *Canadian Social Studies*, 34.4, 2000.

43. David Kilgour, "The Front Line: Human Security and Canadian Foreign Policy," *Canadian Social Studies*, 34.2, 2000.

44. David Kilgour, "The UN and the Challenge of Human Security," *McGill International Review*, 1.1, Winter 2000.

45. Gary King and Christopher Murray, "Rethinking Human Security," *Political Science Quarterly*, Winter 2002, in press, http://gking.harvard.edu/files/hs.pdf, August 21, 2001.

46. Üner Kirdar, "A Trilogy of Basic Human Concerns: Human Rights; Sustainable Human Development; Human Security." *Perceptions, Journal of International Affairs*, III.4 , December 1998-February 1999, http://www.mfa.gov.tr/grupa/percept/iii-4/kirdar.htm, August 23, 2001.

47. Michael Klare, "Redefining Security: The New Global Schisms," *Current History*, 95.604, 1996, pp. 353-358.

48. Edward A Kolodziej, "Renaissance in Security Studies? Caveat Lector!" *International Studies Quarterly*, 36.4, 1992, pp. 421-438.

49. Stephen C Lonergan, Kent Gustavson and Brian Carter, "The Index of Human Insecurity," *AVISO: An Information Bulletin on Global Environmental Change and Human Security*, Issue No. 6, January 2000. Global Environmental Change and Human Security Project, University of Victoria, Victoria, BC, Canada, http://www.gechs.org/aviso/AvisoEnglish/six.shtml, August 24, 2001.

50. S Neil MacFarlane and Thomas G Weiss, "The United Nations, Regional Organisations and Human Security: Building Theory in Central America," *Third World Quarterly*, 15.2, 1994, pp. 277- 295.

51. George MacLean, "Instituting and Projecting Human Security: A Canadian Perspective," *Australian Journal of International Affairs,* 54.3, 2000, pp. 269-275.

52. Sandra J MacLean and Timothy M Shaw, "Canada and New 'Global' Strategic Alliances: Prospects for Human Security at the Start of the Twenty-first Century," *Canadian Foreign Policy,* 8.3, 2001. Abstract available online at http://www.carleton.ca/npsia/cfpj/, August 21, 2001.

53. Jessica Tuchman Mathews, "Power Shift," *Foreign Affairs,* 76.1, 1997, pp. 50-66.

54. Jessica Tuchman Mathews, "Redefining Security," *Foreign Affairs,* 68.2, 1989, pp. 162-177.

55. Anjali Mehta, "Women, Infrastructure and Human Security," *The Radical Humanist,* 58.6, 1994.

56. Abdul Omar, "Challenges of Human Security in Africa," *Peace Magazine,* July 2000, http://www.peacemagazine.org/0007/omar.htm, August 9, 2001.

57. Heather Owens and Barbara Arneil, "The Human Security Paradigm Shift: A New Lens on Canadian Foreign Policy? Report of the University of British Columbia Symposium on Human Security," *Canadian Foreign Policy,* 7.1, 1999, pp. 1-12.

58. Roland Paris, "Human Security: Paradigm Shift or Hot Air?," *International Security,* 26.2, Fall 2001, forthcoming.

59. George Porter, "An Ethical Basis for Achieving Global Human Security," *Development 3,* 1995, pp. 56-59.

60. Cranford Pratt, "Competing Rationales for Canadian Development Assistance: Reducing Global Poverty, Enhancing Canadian Prosperity and Security, or Advancing Global Human Security," *International Journal,* LIV/2, Spring 1999, pp. 306-323.

61. Project Ploughshares, "Human Security and Military Procurement," *Ploughshares Monitor,* June 1999, http://www.ploughshares.ca/content/MONITOR/monj99d.html, August 9, 2001.

62. Vinod Raina, "Rethinking Human Security: Environmental Security in a Globalised Regime," *Asian Exchange,* October 26, 1999, http://www.asianexchange.org/News/94092348326490.php, August 9, 2001.

63. Michael Redclift, "Addressing the Causes of Conflict: Human Security and Environmental Responsibilities," *Review of European Community and International Environmental Law,* 9.1, 2000, p. 44.

64. Laura Reed, "Rethinking Security from the Ground Up," *Breakthroughs,* Spring 2000, pp. 21-27.

65. Ernie Regehr, "Defence and Human Security," *Ploughshares Monitor,* December 1999, http://www.ploughshares.ca/content/MONITOR/mond99a.html, August 9, 2001.

66. Oliver Richmond, "Human Security, the 'Rule of Law' and NGOs: Potentials and Problems for Humanitarian Intervention," *Human Rights Review,* 2.4, 2001, forthcoming.

67. William Rose, "The Security Dilemma and Ethnic Conflict: Some New Hypotheses," *Security Studies,* 9.4, 2000, pp. 1-51.

68. Emma Rothschild, "The Quest for World Order," *Daedalus Journal of the American Academy of Arts and Sciences,* 124.3, 1995, pp. 53-90.

69. Emma Rothschild, "What is Security?," *Daedalus Journal of the American Academy of Arts and Sciences,* 124.3, 1995, pp. 58-59.

70. Ulric Shannon, "Human Security and the Rise of Private Armies," *New Political Science,* 22.1, 2000.

71. Timothy Shaw and Albrecht Schnabel, "Human (In)Security in Africa: Prospects for Good Governance in the Twenty-first Century," *Work in Progress,* A Review of Research Activities of the United Nations University, 15.3, Summer 1999, http://www.unu.edu/hq/ginfo/wip/wipsum99.html#human2, August 28, 2001.

72. Timothy Shaw, "Globalisation and Conflicts in Africa: Prospects for Human Security Development in the New Millennium," *Conflict Trends,* September 1999, http://www.accord.org.za/publications/ct3/global.htm, August 9, 2001.

73. Alex Sherbinin, "Human Security and Fertility: The Case of Haiti," *Journal of Environment and Development,* 5.1, 1996.

74. George Sørenson, "Individual Security and National Security: The State Remains the Principal Problem," *Security Dialogue,* 27.4, 1996.

75. Astri Suhrke, "Human Security and the Interests of States," *Security Dialogue,* 30.3, 1999, pp. 265-276.

76. Larry A Swatuk and Peter Vale, "Why Democracy Is Not Enough: Southern Africa and Human Security in the Twenty-first Century," *Alternatives,* 24.3, 1999.

77. Wigberto E Tananda, "Human Security from a Filipino Perspective," *Peace Review,* September 12, 1999.

78. Ramesh Thakur, "The UN and Human Security," *Canadian Foreign Policy*, 7.1, 1999, pp. 51-59. Abstract available online at http://www.carleton.ca/npsia/cfpj/, August 21, 2001.

79. Richard H Ullman, "Redefining Security," *International Security*, 8.1, 1983, pp. 129-153, 180. United Nations Development Programme (UNDP), "Redefining Security: The Human Dimension." *Current History*, 94, May 1994, pp. 229-236.

81. Hans Van Ginkel and Edward Newman, "In Quest of "Human Security," *Japan Review of International Affairs*, 14.1, 2000, pp. 59-82.

82. Stephen M Walt, "The Renaissance of Security Studies," *International Studies Quarterly*, 35.1, June 1991, pp. 211-239.

83. Douglas Watson, "On Human Security," *Current History*, 95.604, 1996, pp. 392-394.

84. Heidemarie Wieczorek-Zeul, "Security Aspects of Development Cooperation," *Deutsche Stiftung für internationale Entwicklung*, 6, 1999, pp. 8-12.

85. Aaron T Wolf, "Water and Human Security," *AVISO: An Information Bulletin on Global Environmental Change and Human Security*, Issue No. 3, June 1999, http://www.gechs.org/aviso/avisoenglish/three_lg.shtml, August 9, 2001.

86. Susan L Woodward, "Should We Think Before We Leap? A Rejoinder," *Security Dialogue*, 30.3, 1999, pp. 277-282.

87. David Wurfel, "Human Security in East Timor: Xanana's Leadership," *Peace Magazine*, October 1999, http://www.peacemagazine.org/9910/wurfel.htm, August 9, 2001.

www.ingramcontent.com/pod-product-compliance
Lightning Source LLC
Chambersburg PA
CBHW031138270326
41929CB00011B/1676